DISCOVER YOUR TEAM'S POTENTIAL

PROVEN PRINCIPLES TO HELP ENGAGE YOUR TEAM & IMPROVE PERFORMANCE

Featuring insights from: Chris Rollins, Ken Hartley, Kathy Kasten, Jennifer Behan, Wes & Cindy Dove, Beth Reed-Richardson, Ron Cooper, Karen Bemmes, Susan Davis, Matthew Clark, Cherie Dasmacci, Ana Berdecía, Steve Goble, Jelena Simpson, Carla Gray, Jim Costey, Jamie Hansen, Folake Oluokun MD, Gary Belzung, Pamela Quinn, and Melissa Rollins

ROLLINS
PERFORMANCE GROUP
PRESS

Acknowledgments

This book would never have happened without the efforts of so many people. First, I have to acknowledge and thank my wife Melissa, who always supports me when I jump headfirst into a project (often without really knowing what I am getting myself into). I could never accomplish the things I do without her never-ending support.

Regarding the content found within the following pages, each individual contributing author worked diligently to provide insight that the reader will benefit from. They shared from their personal experiences while referencing their training and feedback that many of them have received from working with clients using the DISC Model of Human Behavior to help improve their team's outcomes.

To each author who participated in this collaborative work, I issue a heartfelt THANK YOU to each of you. Your passion for making a positive and lasting impact in our world humbles me. Your drive to keep learning and growing to ensure you are equipped to add value to so many others has provided the fuel that continues to help me study and expand my knowledge as well. The study of human behavior and learning how to help teams achieve peak performance is truly fascinating.

Jennifer Behan, Gary Belzung, Karen Bemmes, Ana Berdecía, Matthew Clark, Ron Cooper, Jim Costey, Cherie Dasmacci, Susan Davis, Wes and Cindy Dove, Carla Gray, Steve Goble, Jamie Hansen, Ken Hartley, Kathy Kasten, Folake Oluokun, Pamela Quinn, Beth Reed-Richardson, Melissa Rollins, and Jelena Simpson, you all never cease to amaze me with your generosity and heart to serve others.

To the hundreds of Human Behavior Consultants in our community that we have trained and certified through the years, each of you is represented in spirit throughout this work. Your ongoing engagement, support, learning, and participation in our DISC community helps everyone continue to grow and develop their skills. There truly is no comparison in the marketplace.

Lastly, I have to acknowledge Dr. Robert Rohm, the Founder of Personality Insights, Inc. When we first connected, I was one of those guys who had "done DISC" before. The training you offered opened my eyes to the true gift that is given to us when we learn to recognize the strengths that lie within every different personality style. For the first time, I moved beyond tolerating other personality styles and learned to honestly celebrate their unique differences without trying to change them. It made me a better leader, and I'm sure it made those I work with happier as well. While I have spent thousands of hours studying human behavior from many sources, including deeply researching the original works of William Marston who created the DISC Model, you had a significant impact in helping develop my passion for becoming a lifelong student of the Model of Human Behavior. I offer my deepest gratitude.

Contents

Introduction

I can't begin to adequately express my excitement in knowing that you have picked up, and started reading this book. I put much thought into developing this collective work. Throughout the coming pages, I will introduce you to a wide variety of authors who have poured their hearts into this work. Each one of them is an expert in their own right.

When approaching the subject of dealing with the Model of Human Behavior that we refer to as DISC, I carefully selected the contributors to this work. I only wanted to include those who could be counted on to deliver not only the thoughts provided here in this book, but also those who were prepared to offer value to their clients at a high level. The last thing I wanted was a group of people who could write something well, but were then ill-prepared to follow up with training when some of you inevitably desire to hire them to help you or your team take your performance to the next level.

With that in mind, deciding where to find the right contributors for this labor of love was an easy one. I speak and train on the DISC Model of Human Behavior across the country. Because this is an open source model, it is easy for people to say they know it well, and to start teaching it to people. The downside is that when I start working with new clients who have had previous exposure to this science, I often have to "un-teach" them some of what they have already learned before they can begin to grasp the concepts in the correct way.

When taught well, this model effectively helps individuals and teams develop the skills necessary to propel their performance to a whole new level; conversely, when it is not taught well, it often causes people to feel labeled, judged, or put in a box. Instead of helping people feel encouraged and understood, some people may feel like there is something wrong with them. If you have ever felt that way after taking a personality assessment, allow me to assure you right now that you have a *wonderful* personality style, wherever you show up on a chart. There is no "ideal" style, and one is not better or worse than another. Trainers who understand this will never leave a member of their audience feeling like they drew the short straw, while unintentionally "over-celebrating" other styles in the room (coincidentally, those tend to be the personality traits most similar to the trainer's own).

The individual contributing authors who are going to share their wisdom with you in the pages ahead all met stringent standards of specific criteria, and all of them have completed the process of becoming Certified Human Behavior Consultants through Personality Insights. While this book is not affiliated with that organization, I chose contributors who have gone through their process. I openly acknowledge that I am a Master Trainer in association with them. The certification classes I hold each year to train people who want to become "DISC Certified" is in conjunction with Personality Insights. However, my *why* regarding this decision is much more critical than my *what*.

Why have I chosen to include these authors in this collective work? These contributors haven't taken some token online class so that they could call themselves "certified". In this day and age, when certifications are often watered down to the point of becoming meaningless, it becomes important to be able to distinguish between those who are "certified" and those who are "qualified". Contributing authors to this book have each completed a minimum of two, full and highly intensive days of in-person training in small group sessions with me. Because I am the Master Trainer who personally trained each of these authors in proper, small group sessions, I can attest to their level of understanding of the model. I don't put fifty people in a class and "lecture" them for two days. I place them in small group sessions where they have to interact not only with me, but with one another, so that they truly understand why people naturally communicate the way they do, and how to adapt to their styles to achieve the connection that improves overall communication. Furthermore, many of the contributors you will hear from have gone through the advanced round of intensive, in-person training to become Advanced Accredited Trainers. When you consider that, along with the fact that they have all had access to over 150 hours of ongoing training and learning beyond the classroom, I believe you will agree that you are going to be learning from the best of the best.

There are some incredible organizations that provide quality assessments and resources, and also follow valid training processes to ensure that those who become certified are equipped to add value to others. I enjoy having in-depth conversations with people who are as passionate about this model as I am, and who have dedicated themselves to becoming efficient and masterful in the art of observing and recognizing this model in action. I know we aren't the only ones who develop quality trainers and consultants with DISC. However, I felt it necessary to include contributors to this book whom I knew well enough to properly vet their abilities to demonstrate a thorough understanding of the DISC Model of Human Behavior.

What you are about to read is not a dissertation of the DISC model itself—there are enough academic books already available on that topic in the marketplace today. Our goal was to share insights from experts who have been applying and teaching this model in their daily personal and professional lives in a way that helps you to read this and say, "I can apply that immediately in my situation."

As you prepare to dive into the pages ahead, I encourage you to take notes, implement the collective wisdom of the experts, and then reach out to them to help bring this life- and culture-changing material into your group or organization.

Chris Rollins

Chapter One

Solving the "Soft Skill" Dilemma

Chris Rollins

Let's address one of the most critical questions you should be asking yourself right out of the gate: How does all of this apply in the real world? You may be thinking something like, *"Talking about people's personality traits is good and all, but that's just a soft skill. We've got real issues to address."* I have heard more variations of that basic phrase than I could count over the years. My response is usually the same every time: "Why do you consider that a soft skill?" When I am told that it is because personality or effective communication isn't measurable, I immediately know that I need to help foster an understanding of the actual difference between a hard skill and a soft skill, as well as bring about an appreciation of the value these skills bring to an organization.

"Soft skills" is a term initially developed by the military to help determine the difference between technical skills and leadership skills, the latter of which are considered equally (if not more) important than the former. The "soft skills" were often harder to teach because when you are dealing with people, it isn't always as simple as telling them to "do this" or "do that." Somehow, along the way, our culture has allowed the term "soft skill" to be thought of as insignificant. Considering that the military began the analysis because they recognized the difference between groups of soldiers achieving victory or defeat often came down to how one group was being led compared to the other, it only makes sense that they decided to devise a system of measuring those leadership skills so that training could be improved in that critical area.[1]

I'm not sure where we lost our way and started thinking these skills weren't measurable, or even relevant. Unfortunately, during the schooling and training process, most students are only subjected to the technical side of a job. They begin to perform their job functions well, then one day, they magically find themselves rewarded with a promotion because the perceived logic is that they should automatically be able to help everyone else perform at the same level. The flaw in this logic is that the criteria for promotion often focuses only on the "hard skills," which are tech driven, while ignoring the "soft skills" which are people driven. The Carnegie Institute of Technology said,

"85% of your financial success is due to your personality and ability to communicate, negotiate, and lead. Shockingly, only 15% is due to technical knowledge."[2]

Study after study has shown that one of the most common causes of involuntary turnover comes from an inability to get along with and effectively lead others. There is so much truth to the old saying, "People are hired for what they know, but fired for who they are."

What can we learn from the military's study? The question remains: "Is a soft skill measurable?" The answer is a resounding YES! The military understood that results are best measured by determining the factors that contributed to the outcome as it related to the overall objective. So, if leadership or communication was to be measured, the measuring stick was to quantify the difference its impact had on mission success. With that understanding, we can certainly measure the impact of soft skills today. The result of ineffective communication, negotiation, and leadership can be seen every day in metrics such as talent acquisition, turnover, employee engagement, morale, customer service scores, sales achievement, safety, and so much more. The common mistake made is when leaders see these results and try to tie everything back to the technical side of training, when in fact, the difference between success and failure is most often linked to effectively communicating in a way that builds a bridge of connection.

What is the ultimate cause of that ineffective communication? And better yet, how can we reverse that trend? Throughout this entire book, many of the contributing human behavior experts are going to share their insights on this very topic. While they are going to share their personal experiences around learning and working with people from all walks of life, my goal is to help lay the foundation that all of them will be working from in each of their chapters. Let's start by addressing the first part of that question.

Why do so many people struggle to communicate and lead effectively? The root of this issue is often miscommunication, which stems from one person not fully grasping the intent or expectation that someone else has for them. As I often say, "they simply aren't speaking the same language."

If I were to stand in front of an audience that spoke another language, I would use an interpreter. That interpreter would know what I was saying, and would then translate what I had just said to the crowd in the language they understood. Just imagine having the superpower of an interpreter who could speak in a language the other person was able to understand! Well, if that intrigues you, welcome to the power of DISC. This language is universal and is spoken around the world. As Nelson Mandela once said, "If you talk to a man in a language he understands, that goes to his head. If you talk to him in his language, that goes to his heart."[3]

I already know the thoughts some of you are having as you read that. You're thinking, "You don't understand, Chris. We both speak the same language and *still* can't get along." I have had 90 percent of my audiences raise their hands when I ask if they felt that concern. Well, this is where we begin to understand why the Model of Human Behavior is so important. Just because we both speak English, for example, does not mean we necessarily speak the same language. *Huh?* Stick with me for a moment...Have you ever thought you understood what someone said to you, and then your take on that information is met with: "That wasn't what I said at all"? The source of that basic miscommunication is the different way in which we all deliver and receive information based on our individual personalities.

When we reference "DISC", the term is synonymous with personality styles. The terminology I tend to use instead is *communication styles*. When you read the phrase "personality style" or "communication style" throughout this book, both terms reference the same thing. The Model of Human Behavior essentially determines the reason why most of us naturally communicate the way that we do. While our goal in this book isn't to spend a significant amount of time covering the academic side of the DISC model, I felt it necessary to provide a brief overview for those who might not be familiar with that terminology.

What is DISC?

The term "DISC" was an acronym originally developed by William Marston in the 1920s to explain the correlation between the emotions that people experience, and the natural influence those emotions have on the way human beings communicate or behave. The original components of Marston's term stand for: Dominance, Inducement, Submission, and Compliance. While each of these four main traits have some very positive character-istics, most of the words have been adapted over the years due to changes in the way words and terms are now used and perceived. The DISC descriptors that many of the contributors to this book will use (that are consistent with the training materials and assessments provided by Personality Insights) are: Dominant, Inspiring, Supportive, and Cautious. Essentially, we measure where someone falls on two sets of scales. The first scale is divided into "Outgoing" or "Reserved". Most people would say they are some of both, but our goal is to determine which trait weighs more heavily on our scale *most of the time*. The second scale is based on "Task" versus "People" orientation. As mentioned before, we all tend to have some of both tendencies, but we typically lean more one way or the other *most of the time*.

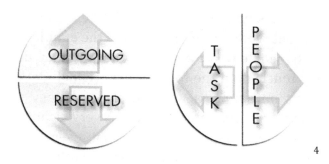

When we merge the two scales, a circle with four quadrants is created. This system forms the basis for determining a person's primary trait of the four measured. In various aspects of life, we find that we tend to move within the entire spectrum and that is perfectly normal, but we usually revert to our primary quadrant; it acts as our personal "home base".

Is DISC something new?

The study of human behavior dates back nearly 2500 years to Empedocles. His study of the four classical elements (earth, water, air, and fire) and how they mixed and intertwined together was the basis for studying and understanding human behavior. Through the years, this study has continued to evolve, just as all forms of psychology, to help us understand human behavior to a greater degree. In the 1920s, Marston designed the concept of DISC, and taught it as a lecturer in college while he developed the model. In 1928, he published the book, *Emotions of Normal People*. He continued the study in the 1931 release of *Integrative Psychology - A Study of Unit Response*, which he co-authored with his wife, Elizabeth H. Marston, and C. Daly King. The basis of this work was to understand the emotions that drive and motivate people to act and react the way they do. While he very briefly touched on the topic in his original work, his study did not focus on abnormal or clinical psychology. While that study is necessary, he wanted to make it very clear that there is nothing wrong with experiencing normal, everyday emotions. They are a part of human behavior that is both observable and predictable.

Is DISC reliable?

Understanding why people tend to behave and communicate the way they do was the whole purpose of Marston's study. He was well aware that people predictably tend to act in certain ways. Because he understood that people's behavior naturally falls into predictable patterns, his goal was to determine which traits were observable, and how they could be measured. The intent was not to label or categorize people, but to better understand them so communication and relationships could be improved. While understanding people is never *foolproof*, science looks at factors using reliability scales to determine validity.

Interestingly enough, after Marston developed the DISC model, he also went on to publish the book, *The Lie Detector Test* in 1938. He had created the systolic blood pressure reading sensor that measured and determined predicable patterns in physical changes that occur when telling a lie versus telling the truth. The lie detector was built on the foundation of DISC.

In essence, DISC measures our "baseline" for how we naturally act. It is never an excuse for acting in a way we shouldn't, and we should never use: "Well, that's just not my style" or "That's just how I'm wired" to excuse bad behavior. Because DISC is intentionally a values-neutral model, it doesn't measure whether someone is good or bad. It is not a model that measures differences between gender, race, religion, age, IQ, education, income, and so forth. Every study I have found to date that even tried to measure those areas for any quantifiable differences between people returned results that measured within the statistical margins of error, suggesting that those factors aren't distinguishable through any of those means.

Regarding the second part of the question I addressed earlier about how we reverse the trend, it comes down to properly training people so they can feel acknowledged for who they are and how they are wired. The goal isn't to make everyone agree, but rather, to ensure that everyone feels understood. Often, I hear people who are going through training respond that it is the first time they felt like someone understood them without trying to *change* them. On that note, you need to know that it is never our goal to try to make someone into something they are not. You were uniquely created, and your personality is perfect just the way it is. The way we reverse the trend of failing to communicate effectively with people is first to learn the dynamics of each particular style, and then to recognize what motivates and encourages people who are high in those traits. After that, it becomes our responsibility to adapt our methods of communication in order to relate to, and lead people the way they need to be related to and led. A leader who says: "Now you know me, so deal with me" is no leader at all.

Allow me to share one final word as you prepare to dive into the incredible insights that await you in the chapters to come. Even though each of the contributors may share their personality styles with you, please understand that we are all a unique blend of all four personality styles. We are never an "either/or" when it comes to DISC. We each have varying intensities of the different traits, and we often flow between styles or adapt to one trait or another as the situation demands. Our purpose is not to determine what we can or can't do, it is more about understanding our natural tendencies as we go through life. I'll share more thoughts on applying this in your daily life in the last chapter. Until then...

ABOUT CHRIS ROLLINS

Chris Rollins is the Founder and President of Rollins Performance Group, Inc., a company that focuses on developing leadership and sales teams to achieve massive top- and bottom-line growth.

He is also a veteran M1A1 tank commander and platoon sergeant. During his sixteen-year corporate career, he led high-performing sales and operational teams in the rental industry, where he became known as "The Sales Train Conductor." He uses his experiences to help his clients learn how to challenge "in-the-box" ideas and concepts in order to achieve "out-of-the-box" results.

Through his impactful keynote presentations, seminar and workshop sessions, books, or consulting clients one-on-one, Chris uses his proprietary 3C Model of Performance as his foundation. The model focuses on the elements of Communication, Connection, and Conversion as the keys to achieving consistent and sustainable growth.

Chris is a Master Trainer in the DISC Model of Human Behavior who has spent thousands of hours studying human behavior and teaching the model to others. He hosts certification classes for those who want to become certified, and better yet, qualified. To learn more about working directly with Chris, please connect at:

Website: https://www.rollinsperformancegroup.com

LinkedIn: https://www.linkedin.com/in/chrisrollins1/

Chapter Two

Are You Multilingual?

Ken Hartley

Posso avere una bottiglia d'acqua per favore?

Μπορώ να έχω ένα μπουκάλι νερό?

Darf ich bitte eine Flasche Wasser haben?

Eu poderia, por favor, ter uma garrafa de água?

¿Puedo por favor tener una botella de agua?

Ok, if you're still scratching your head as to what in the world you're reading, how about this one:

"May I please have a bottle of water?"

I wrote the exact same phrase above in Italian, Greek, German, Portuguese, Spanish, and of course, English. And yes, I can say that in all of those languages, as well as Hebrew and Arabic. Before you become too impressed, that's pretty much the only thing I can say in those languages. That's because water is pretty much the only beverage I drink, so these phrases became a matter of survival when I was traveling in these countries. While I was in France, I said it a few times in French, too, but I can't remember the phrase.

I could have tried English in some of these countries, and it probably would have worked, but if the person I was speaking with didn't speak English too, then it would have been an exercise in futility.

I was once in Nicaragua with a pastor friend. We were in a convenience store buying some soft drinks, and the owners realized my friend was the pastor who was leading a large group of people to their store. They immediately invited him to go behind the store to their house, and sat him in a large recliner and put a fan on him.

He sat there, lounging with his Coca-Cola in hand, looking at the lady of the house, and said, "Your house is beautiful." The woman had a somewhat confused look on her face and shrugged her shoulders, because she only spoke Spanish and didn't have a clue what he had just said to her.

My friend then looked at her and said slowly and with a louder volume, "You... house.... beautiful."

I snickered and whispered to him, "Say it slower and louder. She's gonna get it the next time."

The woman, of course, still had a confused look on her face until I looked at her and said, "Tu casa es muy bonita," to which she smiled broadly and said, "Gracias!"

It didn't matter how slowly or how loudly my friend spoke English to this woman...She only spoke Spanish, and she wasn't going to understand anything else. Why is this relevant? Because as Chris said in the introduction, even though you may be speaking the same verbal language as someone, you may not be speaking the same temperament language. You can slow down, speed up, raise, or lower your volume, but real communication and connection won't happen because you're speaking two different languages!

We already know the four basic temperaments in the DISC model. Each personality has a different language style—a preferred method of communication. If we insist on speaking to someone in our language and expect them to adapt in order to hear us, we are in for a world of hurt with our team members.

There were a few people in my organization that rubbed me the wrong way. I used to think it was their fault, until I heard a certain speaker. Personality Insights Founder, Dr. Robert Rohm, made a powerful statement that changed my life. He said, "We judge others by their actions; we judge ourselves by our intent." For example, when somebody shows up late, our normal first response is to say, "They're always late. That's so disrespectful!"

But when we're late, we say, "Oh, the reason for that was _____" and "I'm not normally this way, but _____ happened," or "Oh, I know I said that, but what I meant was ____." Thus, we give ourselves the benefit of the doubt. We judge ourselves by our intent or what we truly meant, but we don't show others that same courtesy.

When I understood this statement and how each personality temperament wants different things, it opened up a whole new world of communication for me, as well as a deeper understanding of my team members, and even my own family.

Years ago, when I was ten, my father took me to Opryland USA (a theme park) to ride the Wabash Cannonball, a steel rollercoaster with two inversions. I was scared, but my father, knowing my D personality type, asked, "Are you going to let this conquer you?"

I firmly replied, "No!" and got on.

I cried all the way through to the end, at which point my father asked, "What'd you think?"

Looking at him through those tears I replied, "Can we do that again?"

Fast-forward many years, before I knew anything about DISC, to when I took my daughter to Six Flags to ride the Georgia Cyclone, a huge wooden rollercoaster. She was very hesitant. I asked her, "Are you going to let this conquer you?"

She replied, "Yeah." I pressed her to go anyway. She asked me all sorts of questions, giving me a major clue that she was a C personality type, but I ignored those signs.

We got on the coaster, and she cried all the way to the end until, as my father did to me, I looked at her and asked, "What'd you think?"

She screamed, "What kind of parent are you? This is the worst ride ever!" and she stormed off the coaster. I had to catch her, and apologize profusely.

I learned something the hard way that day: different personalities speak different languages, and want different things. (By the way, I'm happy to report that today, my daughter and I ride rollercoasters together.) I had simply messed up by making an assumption that a lot of people make: I speak my type of personality language, and so everyone else must speak it too! However, it's simply not true. Let's briefly look at those different languages...

Of course, the D type language is the easiest for me to speak because I am a D. For those who aren't, let me interpret our language. D types are bottom line people: don't say it in twenty words if you could have said it in five. Our motto is "Be brilliant, be brief, and be gone." We have a ton of things on our plates (by our own doing) and a ton to accomplish. Just give us the highlights of what you need.

I can already hear some of you screaming, "But wait! If I don't tell you every detail, how can you make an informed, correct decision?" Let me help you out here: a D type doesn't need every detail, nor do they want it. They want the absolute, bottom-line, most essential points, and they will make their decision based on that. If you labor on too long with details, their built-in ADD (Attention Deficit Disorder) will have kicked in, and they will check out of the conversation. If they want or need to know more, they'll ask questions.

If you're talking to a D, be *direct* and *to the point*. They'll appreciate it. This is their language!

The I type language is my secondary trait. I am very close to this one too. Their language is fun! Be sure and smile a lot when you talk to them. Remember that they want to be liked! Your smile can make the difference between a fruitful conversation and a dramatic disaster. If you have an entertaining story you can lead with, do it. I types love fun stories! But be ready to patiently listen to the story they will subsequently tell you that will probably "one-up" the one you just told them. Be sure and laugh and tell them how much you enjoyed it. Also, if there is something else they have done well, be sure and commend them on it. I types love positive recognition, especially in front of their peers. Lastly, I types are not detail people. When communicating with them, you want to include how much fun the situation can be and how it can make them look good and be more popular.

If you're talking to an I, be *fun* and *smile*! This is their language!

The S type language is foreign to me. It's my lowest score. I had to learn this language, and it was a labor to do so. Interestingly enough, it also represents the most significant percentage of the population, so if you don't know this language either, you should definitely learn it. S types are far and away the sweetest people you will ever meet. The worst thing you can say to an S is anything in a loud or raised voice. Be conscious of your vocal tones and lower it...especially if you're a D or an I type! Your natural tones of being direct and excited will be intimidating to them. Speak softly and sincerely. Look them in the eyes. Let them know they are appreciated. Remember that they love to know that what they are doing matters and is appreciated. Instead of expressing those affirmations in front of people (that's a big no-no for this temperament), consider writing a handwritten note. They will appreciate it.

If you're talking to an S, be *sincere* and *sweet* and *soft* and choose your words carefully. They are the most *sensitive* of all of the personalities. This is their language!

The C type language is the language of details and efficiency. If you're talking to a C, you'd better have your "ducks in a row" and know what you're talking about. Nothing will elicit a negative response from a C quicker than being wrong in your information, or falsely accusing them of being wrong. Personality types who don't usually give details must learn to provide extensive details when talking to a C. C types are convinced to jump on your team only if they've been given enough correct information to make an informed decision. You'll have to go over all of that information with them and then expect them to ask you for a day or so to think about it while they research what you've told them to make sure it's correct. I used to think this meant they didn't trust me. That's not true. They merely despise being incorrect and want to research everything to make sure they aren't making a mistake. If they do something based on what someone has told them and it turns out to be incorrect information, they will blame themselves for not researching it better much more than they will blame the person who told them something wrong.

If you're talking to a C, be *detailed* and *correct* in your information. This is their language!

My hobby for the last thirty years has been performing as an illusionist. I've been privileged to do this all over the world. I've sawed people in half, levitated audience members, made it snow in the auditorium, and even made a car with spectators around it disappear from the stage and reappear in the parking lot in less than ten seconds. The number one, knee-jerk reaction question I'm asked after every show is, "How did you do that?" While it is the most often asked question, it is also the most trivial question a person could ask, and it's also one a real illusionist/magician will never answer. We know that once the secret is revealed, the magic is over.

But it's more than that...Telling you how a trick is done doesn't help you. You may have a little revelation, but you have no application. For example, I could explain to you in a few seconds how David Copperfield made the Statue of Liberty disappear, but that's simply knowledge. It doesn't mean you could perform the trick in any way, shape, or form, because you couldn't. That takes years of training, honing skills, perfecting presentations, and a lot of money to buy props and advertise. It's so much more than just knowing.

In the paragraphs above, I told you some secrets of communication, but that doesn't mean you can do it. There is so much more to this subject that cannot be covered in one chapter.

That's why you need a specialist in DISC to come in and help you and your organization. And I don't mean someone who watched an online video so they could put a stamp on their profile saying they're "certified." We have immersed ourselves not just in the theoretical study of this material, but also in its practical application. We can help you.

If you want to relate to your team members and have them connect to you, it is imperative that you learn each other's unique personality styles and communicate with them in their primary language. If you need help speaking those languages, consider bringing in one of our Certified Behavioral Specialists to teach you those languages. We're fluent!

Having effective communication with your team means you have to be multilingual. That may be difficult at first, but the rewards you and your team will reap in productivity will make it well worth your investment.

ABOUT KEN HARTLEY

Ken Hartley is an inspirational keynote speaker, an accomplished singer, a talented illusionist, a skilled actor, a published author, and a gifted teacher. He has been a singer and actor on stage and screen since he was five years old. He has also performed as a professional illusionist all over the world, has authored several books, and has released two solo CDs.

As an inspirational speaker and emcee, he has shared the stage with speakers like Rudy Giuliani, Colin Powell, James Smith, Zig Ziglar, and Dr. John C. Maxwell. He loves to encourage and challenge people to overcome limiting obstacles, make leaps and bounds in their personal growth journey, and step into their God-given destinies.

He is a certified Speaker, Trainer, and Coach with The John Maxwell Team as well as an Advanced Certified Human Behavior Consultant with Personality Insights and Dr. Robert Rohm.

He has been in full-time ministry for over thirty years. He currently lives in Tennessee and is married with four children and one grandchild.

To book Ken for your next event, go to
www.hartleyleadership.com.

Chapter Three

Systematic Dynamite + Inspired Team = Masterpiece

Kathy Kasten

If you want to live a fulfilling and successful life as a servant leader, you must be able to interact with others in a way that means something to them. This improved connection can lead to more significant achievements, team bonding, and stronger business value and revenue. Building a network of people with different gifts is a golden key to unlocking treasure chests of potential and possibility—but only if you can understand and interact effectively with each other.

Consider the famous landmark Mount Rushmore, and all of the people who needed to work together to make such a sculpture possible. There was the South Dakota state historian, Doane Robinson, who wrote to sculptor Gutzon Borglum to ask him to consider the idea. There were those who trained and encouraged Gutzon before his work on Mount Rushmore. There were the people who funded the project, people who physically worked on the project, Gutzon's son, Lincoln, who finished the project, a state park staff of people who still care for the monument, visitors who appreciate the project, people who market the monument...[1] You get the idea.

The monument in the mind of one person was just an idea. It took a fantastic team across decades to make that idea a reality. The title of this chapter alludes to each of the four basic personality styles in DISC: "Dynamite" for the "D" drive-gifted people, "Inspired" for the "I" persuasive-gifted people, "Team" for the "S" patience-gifted people, "Systematic" for the "C" perfectionist-gifted people. Added together, they created a masterpiece that will last for generations.

Early in my career, I worked in management for a Fortune 500 company. One day, I was called into a division leader's office and told that a major client was unhappy. Our company was receiving hundreds of frustrated phone calls, and the client was considering putting an end to their business dealings with us. I had no knowledge or direct contact with this customer, but our division leadership believed that I could untangle this potentially disastrous situation and bring it to a successful resolution. I was given 24 hours to find and fix the problem.

Understanding human behavior and having a topnotch, previously built network was critical to me in those 24 hours. I could not have found and fixed the problem alone. I needed knowledge and strengths that I did not possess. With the varied skills of our team, we were able to solve the issues of hundreds of people, show resolve as a company to make things right in a bad situation, and demonstrate the strength of our employees both to our client, and to our own company leaders.

A quality network is critical, and is something I believe in so profoundly that I built an online course to help others find the "right" people for the "right" time. But in addition to selecting the right people, you need to be able to understand and connect with them.

Why can't we just be a team? Does it really matter if we understand each other well? To think about those questions for a moment, let's imagine four people, each of whom speaks only their native tongue: Malay, Norwegian, Japanese, and Greek. How do we connect? How do we get past even elementary communication and achieve great results? Whatever we attempt will be complicated, and filled with many hand gestures and frustration. Now imagine that same team with a single interpreter who can help all of us understand each other better...What would such an interpreter be worth?

When we try to interact with others who have different personality styles, it can be an experience similar to crossing world language barriers.

Perhaps one of the most effective tools I have been given in my search to understand human behavior better—both mine and those I serve—has come about through the Personality Insights DISC advanced human behavior training. It has opened new worlds to me, to my family, and to companies and individuals I work with in my life.

Many people may feel misunderstood, unappreciated, or just stuck. A reserved person may feel overlooked or left behind. An outgoing person may feel that others don't take them seriously. A driven person may have a great idea, but can't seem to get traction to take it anywhere. A careful person may have important details to share, but feels that no one wants to listen to them.

We often gravitate toward those who are similar to us. We understand them; we connect easily with them. I am a D/SC on the DISC model. I am driven and excited to reach new heights, try new ideas, set big goals, and build great networks. I love a challenge and accomplishing what seems impossible. As a person who has a multifaceted leadership background, I am good at team building, marketing, leadership, coaching, and networking. I want to serve others using what I have learned. Because of my personality style, I enjoy talking with other driven idea generators.

But I am limited by time, space, and resources. I need the strengths of others in areas that are more challenging for me. If I want to reach beyond today and bring a big idea into existence successfully, I need help from detail people, persuasive people, and reliable people.

I also tend to be reserved. I will often spend a few quiet days recharging after I lead or speak at an event. In my world, outgoing people who propose a spontaneous dinner just to laugh and relax are perplexing. *What? Not do something? Not plan the next big idea? Not schedule the meal for the optimum time? Not be knee-deep in books and ideas relating to the next 25 years?* In DISC, those perplexing people demonstrate "I" tendencies, my most challenging gift style.

I distinctly remember a day when I was at a training event and we took a break for lunch. I had traveled alone but ended up going to lunch with three "I" personalities. They were laughing, conversing, hugging, talking with the staff, taking selfies, and bubbling over with excitement. I was getting exhausted just watching them! But they reminded me of something valuable that day: they helped me to reconnect with the importance of fun, laughter, and bonding just for the sheer delight of it. I had been so focused on reaching goals that I was missing out on too much of the joy in the journey.

As I assessed my inner circle, I realized that I had very few of these amazing people in my daily life. They bring important and valuable assets to the table. I now make a point of spending more time with "I" types. I am thankful for them. I am learning to appreciate and understand their gifts at a deeper level. I wonder how many times we ignore or dismiss those who have gifts different than our own.

My entire family—from my parents to my grandchildren—has taken the DISC profile. Even though we have spent our entire lives interacting, we learned so much about each other from that experience. We have learned better ways to communicate with each other based on our behavioral tendencies.

An example of that occurred with another parent within my family that is a very High D. They are creative, driven, determined, out-of-the-box minded, and goal focused. One of their children is a C child. This child is meticulous when building with toys, likes to follow instructions, organizes by category and color, takes time to think things through, and wants to do things right. When the D parent asked their child to clean their room in a single statement, the child felt overwhelmed, and would become highly stressed. *"What part of the room should I do first?"* *"Is it okay if the toys are just in the container, or do you want them sorted in a certain way?"* *"What process do you want me to follow?"* *"What exactly does a clean room look like?"* *"Can you define how I know when I am done?"*

It could be natural to assume the child just didn't want to clean their room. (That may be part of it.) But with DISC training and understanding comes the realization that this child needs sequence, clear expectations, and time to process. A D-style broad and direct goal statement does not provide enough information in the C-style child's world, thus causing a mental shutdown. Imagine how much better this situation became for both parent and child once the D parent learned to speak in the child's behavioral language.

In another instance, I was working with a client whose business connected daily with end consumers. After some initial information gathering, I suggested that all of the upper management team take DISC profiles to determine the strengths and needs of the team. Through the assessments, we discovered that the management team was missing High I-styled leaders—the very type of leaders that would most identify as outgoing and people oriented. And yet, their very business depended on great interaction with people.

This discovery led to a decision by management to look for and hire outgoing and people-oriented leaders. They asked final job candidates to take a DISC profile to help them determine who might bring those skill sets to the table.

Additionally, I led DISC leadership and team training for the current and primarily reserved leadership so they could learn how to better interact with others who had an outgoing style. I created a team chart that reflected the current behavior styles represented. I also did interactive two-person reports that allowed those involved to understand each other better and learn ways to interact more effectively. Imagine the potential and strength that was added to the company and leadership team with this fresh perspective.

I want to champion each person in his or her pursuit to be their best. I am guessing that you care about that too...That is why you are reading in this book. It is so rewarding to share in someone's journey as they see new possibilities, learn to truly connect with others in an area that they are passionate about, or begin working more effectively with their team to achieve amazing goals with their God-given abilities. Doesn't it feel great when we are fulfilled, serving others, and doing what we love to do?

I have been blessed with many wonderful mentors and teammates over the years. I have benefited from the advice of high achievers who have gone before me. I have applied many ideas and suggestions that have produced exciting results. And I have made mistakes that could have been avoided had I sought out and benefited from the gifts of others. DISC, properly applied, is a powerful resource. Here are a few tips to help you in your leadership growth journey. Implementing even one of them will take you closer to the goals and relationships you desire.

TIP 1: See yourself from the outside in. Take one of the DISC profiles. These profiles are available for, and tailored to many different areas, including leadership, personal, sales, fitness, children, and more. A DISC profile is an essential first step to more fully understanding your own behaviors. Personality Insight's DISC profiles are positive, encouraging, and personalized. You will find a new perspective.

TIP 2: Have team members take DISC assessments. Whether you are involved with a board, a management team, your family, or a group of friends, the insights from DISC assessments can take your connections to a whole new level.

TIP 3: Incorporate ongoing DISC training/growth days into your schedule. Think about how much time, stress, and money you will save. Many authors of this book have put hundreds, and even thousands of hours into learning about DISC behaviors, and we are still learning. The more you learn and practice, the better at effective interaction you will become.

TIP 4: Consider Two-Person Interactive Reports: CEO/ HR Manager; Parent/child; Entrepreneur/marketing team; Pastor/Elders. The stronger the team, the better the results.

TIP 5: Make a list, mind map, or vision board of three great things you want to accomplish in your life, or with your team. Which "good" things you can let go of in order to get to those "great" things? Set measurable goals. When will they be accomplished? How will you know when you have arrived at your desired destination? Take a small step each day toward one of those great things, and before you know it, you will have reached your goal.

Investing in your potential and the potential of others by taking DISC assessments can have measurable results and create greater harmony. In the end, you are not connecting with yourself, you are connecting with others. You need to learn to speak in their language. Begin today. I am excited for you. I can't wait to hear and celebrate your successes!

ABOUT KATHY KASTEN

Kathy Kasten is the CEO, Founder, and President of Lion Crest Leadership LLC, a company focused on maximizing leadership potential for high-achieving individuals and organizations who want to reach extraordinary results and enjoy greater fulfillment, personally and professionally.

Kathy's background in varied spheres (multiple small business owner, Fortune 500 management, managing homeschooled teenage daughter's 10,000-books-sold writing career) allows her to bring a high level of excellence and a unique perspective to those she serves. She has worked with businesses, foundations, entrepreneurs, retirees, students, non-profits, educators, local government, and communities, adding value in areas such as leadership and team development, personal growth, business culture, customer service, marketing, sales, strategic planning, goal setting/achievement, and legacy.

Kathy works with her clients to heighten their understanding and ability to successfully leverage personal and organizational gifts through leadership and team development conferences and training, workshops, keynote presentations, online courses, assessments, executive coaching, books, and DVDs.

Kathy lives in Minnesota, is happily married to her high school sweetheart, and has one child and four beautiful grandchildren. She is also an Advanced DISC Certified Human Behavior Consultant.

To learn more about working directly with Kathy, please connect her at:

Website: https://www.lioncrestleadership.com

LinkedIn: https://www.linkedin.com/in/kathykasten/

Chapter Four

Finding Your Career Fit

Jennifer Behan

What do you want to be when you grow up? What are you going to study in college? What are you going to do with that degree? These are questions that many of us have either asked or been asked sometime in our life. Some of us have found great satisfaction in our careers, while others find themselves searching for something different. Why do some seem to find the right fit while others move on to something other than what they studied in college? Obviously, most people choose their careers because it's what they are interested in. Sometimes, though, this is not enough. We all have a unique personality style, which I believe can be overlooked or undervalued in the process of choosing a career. Being aware of our personality style and how that affects everything we do can have a profound impact on the profession we select and, ultimately, our satisfaction in life.

When I was young, I enjoyed playing school with my friends, and my favorite part was being the teacher. I liked being up front, talking and teaching. When I was in high school, I was pretty good at math and thought, "I'll be an accountant." It took my first college math class to change that idea for me! That same year, I completed a basic nutrition course and loved it. It was fascinating to me, and while others complained about how hard it was, I found it quite easy to understand. That set my course to become a registered dietitian.

After getting my first job in a hospital working with heart and physical rehab patients, I began to get frustrated and bored with my job. There were many times doctors did not see the professional value of what dietitians offered their patients other than hospital food selection and diet instructions. I enjoyed meeting people and talking to them, but taking away their desserts and counseling them to change their fifty-year-old eating habits did not really make them happy, and in turn, didn't make me happy. I didn't like being "the bad guy" and was bored with giving the same diet instructions to most of my patients. Furthermore, I never got to see the outcome of my counseling after patients left the hospital...Had I made a difference in their lives?

A few years later, I was introduced to DISC, and it began to make sense why I was dissatisfied with my dietetics career and never wanted to go back to it after having children. I had chosen a career based solely on what my interests were and what I was good at instead of looking at my personality style and how the daily tasks would fit with my behavior style and what kept me motivated. I also did not recognize my need/desire to be valued as a professional within the hospital setting. I believe an awareness of what type of environment one thrives in based on one's needs, wants, values, motivations, and behavior style dramatically impacts a person's satisfaction and success within a chosen career. The key is finding out what that environment is and how to apply that to your career goals.

Step 1: What Is Your Pace?

Two of my children are fast-paced. They talk fast; they think fast; they act fast (sometimes to their detriment). My other child is slow-paced. He thinks things through, doesn't have a lot to say, and is slow and steady when walking from place to place. How about you? Are you fast-paced or slow-paced? Do you like things to move quickly or slowly? Fast-paced people tend to make decisions rapidly, taking the information they have and moving forward. If you are slower-paced, you like to take your time making decisions, reviewing the information thoroughly and cautiously making a decision. You might be somewhere in the middle, but keep this factor in mind when choosing a career. If you are fast-paced and choose a career where the daily activity is slow-paced, it might drive you crazy. You will want to scream: "People, can you just make a decision and move on?" On the other hand, if the career you choose features fast-paced daily activity and you are slow-paced, you may find yourself stressed out on a regular basis.

Step 2: What Is Your Priority?

My dad loves to cook. If you walk into the kitchen when he's working, he'll say hello and keep stirring the pot. My mom loves people. When we walk in, she gets distracted from what she's doing, gives us a hug, and begins to talk to us. Are you task-oriented (like my dad) or people-oriented (like my mom)? If you are task oriented, you value getting things done more than being with people. A people-oriented person values being around and working with others. Another way of figuring this out is by asking what gives you energy and what drains you. A task-oriented person gains energy by getting things done and checking things off their list. A people-oriented person gains energy just by being around others. For example, I had an organizer come and help me sort through my house. After two hours, I had a headache, was tired, and was ready to be done. My organizer said to me, "I'm just getting started! Drink some coffee and let's go!" Obviously, she was a task-oriented person, and I am people oriented. Someone who is task-oriented may have a difficult time working with lots of people, or it might leave them stressed out and exhausted at the end of the day. If you are a people-oriented person, consider choosing a career that involves working with lots of people. Of course, every job will have tasks to complete, but a people-oriented person is going to need lots of interactions with other people to keep them going. My very people-oriented son briefly considered a job fixing computers. After I explained to him that much of the work would involve being alone and possibly working on one task for a long time, he realized that sort of career would not be the best fit for him.

Step 3: Challenges, Conflict, and Confrontation with Others

As a dietitian, there were several times when I would have to contact the doctor because they had written the wrong diet prescription, or I disagreed with their orders. This was not something I enjoyed, because I am not one who enjoys confrontation. How do *you* deal with challenges, conflict, and confrontation? Do you like to be challenged by others, or are you more comfortable with the status quo in order to keep the peace? Challenges can bring change, and there are those who love that! Others, though, prefer things to stay the same, because change brings stress. Some people do not mind conflict; in fact, it energizes them. Others prefer a peaceful, non-conflict atmosphere where getting along is valued. Is the career you are looking into one that will present a high amount of challenge that will need to be addressed through confrontation? If yes—is this something you are comfortable with, or will it bring stress, and be difficult for you? Different careers present different challenges, conflicts, and confrontations to our lives, and understanding how we deal with them can help us decide which career to pursue.

Step 4: Environmental Needs

We all thrive in different environments. Some people need the freedom to do their work without constant supervision, direction, and questions. They prefer to be in charge and get things done so they can move on to the next project. Others desire an environment that provides clear direction in their daily tasks, plenty of time to get things done correctly, management that listens and addresses their questions, and long-term goals that allow for planning and accuracy. Another person might need an environment that gives them recognition, allows for friendly relationships to develop, encourages people to verbalize their ideas, and provides opportunities to influence and inspire others. Finally, some people prefer an environment that is stable, secure, and consistent, usually specializing in one area of work with an established pattern, while finding joy in being part of a group.

Step 5: Details, Details, Details!

One of my favorite movies is *Mr. Mom*. There's a line where the dad is asked what type of electrical voltage he was going to put in the house. His answer was, "Two twenty, two twenty-one; whatever it takes." Obviously, this guy was not detail oriented. What about you? Do you like to dig in and work on the details, or do you prefer to be involved in the bigger picture, leaving the details to someone else? Some careers involve lots of details, precision, and micromanaging. This can require intense focus, often necessitating staying the course until the project is done. Others may instead prefer to be the one who casts the vision, sets the goals for others, encourages the team, and then lets them figure out the details. If you are not one who thrives on details and isn't concerned about getting things exactly right, then I would avoid choosing a career that demands that details and numbers be perfect.

Step 6: Short-Term or Long-Term Goals

I am a great starter, but not so great at finishing! I have grand ideas of what something is going to wind up like, but have many projects that are halfway done. Do you have someone in your life like this? If you prefer long-term goals, you are probably one who likes details, can focus on one thing for long periods of time, and methodically plans and executes well. On the other hand, if you prefer short-term goals, you probably like a lot of variety, are prone to becoming bored quickly, and enjoy coming up with new ideas. Again, keep this in mind when choosing a career.

Step 7: Putting It All Together

As you read through this material, you may find that you feel you can be both one and the other. In other words, you may be task-oriented or people-oriented, depending on the situation. That's normal, but I encourage you to figure out which areas describe you more often. For instance, I can be detail-oriented and focused in some areas of my life (for a short period), but most of the time, I am not detail-oriented. You might be able to pick up the pace when you need to, but you might not want a job that is fast-paced if you tend to be slower-paced more often. Ultimately, it is your decision, so if you are looking at a career that seems to pull from the traits that are not your strengths, understand that this may cause stress and burnout. There will always be things we have to do that we aren't good at, but choosing a career that fits most of your behavior style traits can help increase satisfaction and fulfillment in your life.

What does this look like in real life? I was helping a boy named John figure out what he might want to study in college. John was fast-paced, people-oriented, loved being recognized, had a difficult time staying focused for long periods, always gave words of encouragement, enjoyed being creative, and was hesitant in a confrontation. After reviewing his choices, I was surprised to see he had chosen architecture as a career option. Being an architect is a slower-paced job, would require both attention to detail, and working on long-term projects, and would entail working alone for much of the time. As we dug deeper, John realized that what interested him about being an architect was the creativity and look of the final project. Another career that piqued his interest was owning a landscape architect company. This seemed to fit John better. He could run a fast-paced business, work daily with staff, as well as clients, use his creativity in designing, but pass on much of the details of the project to others while he moved on to build his clientele.

Looking back at my career, I understand why I chose it. I found nutrition fascinating, and I did enjoy meeting and interacting with people. What I didn't realize was that the job would come with a lack of variety, as well as trying to encourage people to change what they aren't excited about, and not knowing if what I was doing made a real difference in people's lives long-term. No career is perfect and will meet every aspect of your personality style strengths; thankfully, though, once you better understand your unique personality and the needs, values, environmental style, and motivations that come with it, you will be better equipped to make an informed decision. I wish you all the best in finding your best career fit!

ABOUT JENNIFER BEHAN

Jennifer Behan is the owner of J Behan Consulting, a company that trains people to understand their unique personality style and communicate more effectively with others in order to help them work better together and achieve their desired results. She is an Advanced DISC Certified Human Behavior Consultant as well as a registered dietitian. Her experience includes counseling individuals, teaching classes, and speaking to community groups, as well as training teachers, parents, students, and business owners.

Jennifer enjoys working with high school and college students, helping them navigate the wide field of majors and career choices in order to draw out what they really want to do sooner rather than later in life. Higher education can be costly; it is her desire to help students truly understand who they are in order to more effectively utilize their time and money in pursuing a career that is fulfilling and satisfying.

To learn how to work directly with Jennifer, you can contact her at:

Website: https://www.jbehanconsulting.com

Email: jennifer@jbehanconsulting.com

Chapter Five

After Two Decades, We Understand!

Wes and Cindy Dove

We spent the first twenty years of our lives together raising our kids and climbing our respective corporate ladders. Like many other couples, we butted heads from time to time. We usually wrote off these disagreements as simple misunderstandings. There were indeed plenty of times when we told the kids one thing, but they heard another. And there were more than a few times when those simple misunderstandings had the potential for waking the neighbors!

Our corporate lives were different, but not that different! A significant portion of Cindy's corporate career was with a large, local healthcare organization. For the bulk of that time, she reported directly to one manager, and that department ran smoothly with minimal turnover. When a giant national conglomerate bought out that company, everything changed rapidly! And through the years of training employees on the concepts of behavior-based safety and various other corporate safety and HR initiatives, I (Wes) had the opportunity to watch people with varying degrees of education and technical skills experience incredibly different levels of success—which was rarely tied directly to tenure or a degree.

Through all the ups and downs, personal or professional, one thing stood out more than any other: when communication was clear, things just went more smoothly. Unfortunately, like most everyone around us, we were never really able to *put a finger on* what made some situations really good and others really bad.

The inverse was also true...There were plenty of times where it seemed like we were speaking an entirely different language than the person we were communicating with. I would typically have the end in mind as we started any project around the house, but Cindy would have what felt like an enormous number of questions. As we raised our kids, a stern look of disapproval would often bring Renee to tears, while Matthew wanted to control every situation.

We saw that pattern continue in our professional lives as well. One employee would get promoted into a supervisory role and be able to connect with their entire team, while another person, just as technically competent, could alienate a whole department within days of accepting their new position. Our peers would sometimes be on waiting lists to work for one manager while there didn't seem to be enough money in the budget to staff another manager's department, even when the workload was actually lighter.

In nearly fifteen years of teaching the concepts and practical application of behavior-based safety across North America, and helping position the facility I worked in on a daily basis to have the most effective behavior-based safety process within that global company, I had taken a drawerful of assessments and had studied human behavior and temperaments six ways from Sunday. All of that helped me to develop a deeper understanding of my own strengths and weaknesses, and even how I was wired internally, but nothing I had seen gave me real insight into how I could translate that into the work I was doing, or how to communicate better with the people I trained.

During this same time, as Cindy's career in healthcare grew, she noticed a culture of intentional distance and disconnection from those in leadership positions toward their patients, and in many cases, their direct and supporting staff as well. While we all understand boundaries, the choice to only communicate the facts—as opposed to intentionally connecting with patients and families on a human level—had significant consequences, often resulting in the lack of relatability for all parties involved. As we've become more connected as a society through social media and other avenues, Cindy has noticed an increased strain on the healthcare field in areas where a more relational approach to connecting with patients and staff has not been adopted. In areas where it has, she finds engaged patients who are absorbing the close communication, thus enabling them to better care for themselves. In addition, she finds happier staff and doctors.

We all expect our physician to be personable at some level; physicians generally lose patients when they're not willing to take this approach. To make this challenge more pronounced in the healthcare field, you will typically see the nursing field attract a high degree of the C or CS blend personality where procedure, standards, and critical thinking are essential. Bring the S into play along with the C personality, and you have a blend of a critical thinking, supportive, and relational individual caring for you or your loved one._While doctors often share the High C style, many also tend to have a high mix of D in their blend. With this double-task focus, their communication can come across as very matter-of-fact, and can quickly alienate a patient and their family at a critical time. The nurses then seem to catch the brunt of that family's frustration!

It wasn't until Cindy transitioned from operations—dealing primarily with clinical staff and senior level administrators—into a sales and marketing role in the senior living field where she helped families make significant decisions on how to best care for their aging parents, that she recognized how important providing every detail with a genuinely caring approach could be! And while she didn't associate it with her C/SD blend at the time, she can look back now and realize how that detailed and caring approach allowed each family to process the information, and how it earned their trust in what was almost always a challenging transition for them and their loved ones.

When I toured a work site in order to benchmark production processes and safety initiatives, I saw something that may actually have an impact on how people could communicate more effectively with one another. And it all boiled down to some simple stickers on their hard hats...I also don't believe that it was a coincidence that we met Chris Rollins, and started a mentoring relationship around that same time!

In the months that followed, we dove head first into the DISC Model of Human Behavior. This remarkably simple tool opened our eyes to so many things we could both do daily to become more effective! Through nearly eighty hours of face-to-face instruction, and countless additional hours virtually, Chris unlocked a whole new level of understanding, almost all of which was there intuitively all along, by teaching us the simplicity behind the Personality Insights curriculum.

Now it made complete sense that my drive for results and focus on the big picture (mixing some fun and attention to detail in along the way) was a function of my D/IC behavioral style blend. And when Cindy had so many questions about the details and would sometimes get overwhelmed by that constant drive, it tied directly back to her C/SD style blend. As a High S/I blend, we realized just how much those stern looks threatened Renee's need for peace and harmony. And it also helped us understand why Matt would so frequently challenge us for control when we saw that he shared my D/IC style blend!

Having assessment results that gave us simple, yet incredibly accurate feedback on how we were each wired to behave and communicate, both on cruise control and under stress, certainly opened the door to becoming more effective. But the real results, in our family lives and in *every* professional situation, really started showing up as we dug deeper into that curriculum. This gave us a solid understanding of how to quickly recognize the primary communication styles of the people we were working with, and more importantly, a platform for adapting our own communication so that we were speaking the language they could best understand. We also learned that having this knowledge made it our responsibility to apply it, regardless of whether the other person knew it or not.

While we were still working full-time in the corporate world, not only were we able to use this new understanding to be more effective in our own roles, we were also able to help those companies begin to provide large parts of their workforce with this same understanding!

For example, in healthcare, the way a message is given to a patient or their family is often even more important than the message itself. In manufacturing, achieving peak productivity is often more about expressing the goal in terms each team member understands than cracking the proverbial whip. And what construction company wouldn't benefit from tailoring its message in terms specific to each customer? But regardless of the industry, employee engagement is improved, and retention is significantly higher when the messages we're sending are actually received! All of those things can be addressed immediately as an organization's leaders begin applying these tools based on the DISC Model of Human Behavior.

In almost every culture, there's some sort of reference to what we know as "The Golden Rule": *Do unto others as you would have them do unto you.* While we'd certainly never challenge the source, applying it in the most literal sense as it relates to how we communicate with one another may cause some challenges. If Wes uses his "charge the finish line" approach each time he talks with Cindy, simply because that's how he would like to be treated, she will quickly feel overrun. And if Cindy provides Wes with every detail to every scenario, since that leads to the level of accuracy she values, he may quickly lose interest entirely.

Chris taught us an alternate thought on that concept—the idea of a "Platinum Rule": *Do unto others as they would have you do unto them, based on their unique style.* By adapting our message to the communication style we recognize in the people we're interacting with, not only do we have a much better chance of them actually understanding, but we send the message that we value their uniqueness, and what they can contribute!

As we work with different organizations and teams, many of which are in those industries we connected with throughout our corporate careers, we love seeing the expressions on the faces of the supervisors and managers as they begin to "get it"! Not only does this almost always have an immediate impact on increasing productivity and eliminating the common errors that come from simple misunderstandings, but it can also transform the atmosphere for every employee they work with! Whether unemployment numbers are at an all-time high or an all-time low, the best companies always want to attract and retain the best people. And regardless of how strong the economy is at any given time, those same companies will certainly prefer high profitability to lower profitability ten times out of ten!

When we're able to help an organization to begin applying the DISC Model of Human Behavior as a part of their culture, the needle starts to move immediately. These simple tools provide up-and-coming team members—so many of whom we've seen struggle as they've moved from their roles as individual contributors into roles where they're responsible for a group of people—with tangible action items they can apply right away. By looking for the answers to two simple questions, a new supervisor/manager/leader can identify, with a high degree of accuracy, the primary communication style of each person for whom they're responsible, and adapt their communication so that those team members can receive it in their own terms. And when they take that extra step of implementing the world-class assessment tools we can help them with through Personality Insights, those leaders get a detailed understanding of how their team members tick—and how they're likely to respond in different ways in times of stress.

These last two decades have taught us a lot. There have certainly been some successes we're proud of, and we've done our best to learn from the many mistakes we've made along the way. But realizing that most of the lessons we've learned would have been much simpler if we'd had this understanding of the Model of Human Behavior from the beginning serves as a driving force for us to pass this message on to every individual or organization that we can. Our hope is that it will allow their leaders to learn from our errors so they can make a positive impact on people we may never meet!

So, if productivity, profitability, engagement, or retention matter in your organization, we'd challenge you to figure out how quickly you can build a practical application of the DISC

Model of Human Behavior into your culture! And if you want to build great relationships with each person you care about in your personal life, we haven't seen a better way of doing this than learning to really value their unique style, and speaking the language they best understand. We know firsthand how much the tools from this amazing DISC platform have helped us in terms of achieving remarkable results in every aspect of our lives. The same can happen for you, if you'll just dive into it!

ABOUT WES & CINDY DOVE

Prior to founding Dove Development & Consulting, Wes and Cindy Dove developed strong professional resumes while working in both large corporations and small, family-owned businesses. In addition to extensive work in behavior-based safety throughout North America, Wes was responsible for safety compliance, human resources, and personnel development in multiple industries.

In over twenty years in the healthcare field, Cindy was responsible for operations, hospice, and sales. By applying a foundation of leadership and effective workplace communication principles, Cindy created high levels of success for the companies she served.

Both Wes and Cindy are Executive Directors with The John Maxwell Team, serve on that organization's President's Advisory Council, and are Certified Human Behavior Consultants through Personality Insights.

Their primary focus is helping others fulfill the kinds of needs they personally experienced in their careers and also watched great organizations struggle with while attempting to develop the "soft skills" of their up-and-coming leaders. By providing practical tools for immediate implementation, Wes & Cindy help teams overcome some of the biggest roadblocks preventing their clients from achieving peak performance and profitability in their workplace. To learn more about working directly with them, they can be contacted at wes@dove-development.net or cindy@dove-development.net or by visiting their website: https://dove-development.net/

Chapter Six

That's Not My Job

Beth Reed-Richardson

Have you ever been sitting at work and overheard someone say, "That's not my job!" Well, you're not alone: that statement is made way too often in the workplace. There are various reasons why someone might make that comment, but the idea is that they are disengaged. Not only can disengaged employees create a negative work environment, but they can also cause a company to lose money.

According to a Gallup poll, actively disengaged employees cost US companies between $450 - $550 billion in lost productivity per year.[1] For an organization to reach its real potential and carry out its mission, the employees must be engaged, and every team member must be proficient and productive. Having been in customer service for over twenty years, most of the team members that I've seen who were disengaged, not proficient, or not productive in their roles were the same team members who would make some of the following statements: "That's not my job," "I don't feel supported," "Nobody trained me," or "I should have gotten that promotion."

Many of these statements are made because there is a lack of communication, clarification, or understanding of what the team member needs, or how their role impacts the overall success of the company or organization. "That's not my job" is an attitude that will kill your career because it does not foster a team environment, and likely, does not reflect your company's mission, vision, or values. It paints the picture that you're not willing to help your co-workers when they need a hand. I consider this possibly one of the worst things you could say to your peers or manager. Unfortunately, for years, I didn't ask the most critical question of all... Why would the team members make any of those statements?

Although I have been very successful throughout my career, my accomplishments came with a lot of trial and error. It was almost like I was hitting a brick wall at times because early in my career, I was not aware of my own unique personality. I didn't realize that others might misunderstand or misread my actions. I often didn't ask the questions I needed to and might not have always taken the time to listen to, or consider what others might have to say. I had a ton of energy, but not everyone loves the excitement of change and variety as much as I did. If I had known more about the personalities of each team member when I first became a manager, then we would have been able to achieve our goals much quicker. I was successful, but it took two to three times longer than it did once I had a better understanding of my personality strengths as well as those of my team members. I have seen team members excel once they have learned to embrace their strengths and capitalize on the strengths of those around them.

I helped a team ranked in the bottom 10 percent of a Fortune 500 Company reach the top 10 percent in profitability within two years by taking them through the DISC assessment and team training. The team was willing to utilize the tools to learn how to communicate better with each other and help identify strengths that would ultimately benefit them. It was almost like seeing a light bulb go off when I tapped the personality strengths of each leader. A perfect example of utilizing strengths was when a more supportive leader helped a more dominant leader role-play a difficult performance discussion. This ensured the leader was prepared to have the conversation with open dialogue and accurate understanding of the needs of the team member versus just telling them what they had observed. That did not happen before the leaders completed the assessment and went through various trainings.

Even today, after hundreds of hours of training and development in the study of human behavior from various organizations, I still have to step back and think about how I'm communicating with others, and how they could perceive what

I'm trying to say or do. We are all human, and I definitely agree with Lukas Herrmann that there is truth to the saying, "You need to know yourself to understand other people."[2] Each of us has strengths, but being supportive is something that I have had to really focus on over the years.

Depending on our personality style or talents, each of us has things that motivate us or inspire us differently. I love to WIN! It doesn't matter if it's a mountain bike race, a friendly competition, or if I'm trying to achieve a goal. It's not about the recognition for me, it's about the feeling of success and knowing that I accomplished something I set out to do. This has driven me throughout my career and has allowed me to received recognition for increased associate engagement and productivity, providing a WOW experience for our customers, and delivering top and bottom-line performance throughout numerous organizations.

I remember reading the book *The How of Wow*, which focused on how you create raving fans—customer advocates who go out of their way to spread the right word about the experiences they have consistently had with you.[3] I definitely agree that we need to create fans out of the customer, and I was fortunate to have leaders who took it one step further and encouraged me to ensure my team members felt the same way about how the team was treated.

I once led a team that had been through several different managers before I joined the organization. They had not had the support they needed, and didn't feel like they were appreciated. I had heard over and over again that they used to love working for the company, but many of them were frustrated with their current situation and ready to quit. I decided to take some time and get to know my new team. I started making weekly calls, more frequent visits with their locations, and scheduled leadership meetings. At that time, as a district manager, I had over twenty-five locations in two different states, and I was not always able to make it to their offices. I knew the most important thing I could do was be consistent with each leader and have one-on-one conversations which would allow me to find out more about their strengths and how I could help best support them. During those conversations and weekly planning meetings, I soon realized there were so many people who had the capacity, potential, and ability to do beautiful things within and for the organization, but they had been somewhat neglected and never heard the simple words, "Thank you," or "How can I help you?"

How can an organization or leader expect a team member to be engaged if he or she is not being recognized, supported, or encouraged? Jack Welch said it best: "There are only three measurements that tell you nearly everything you need to know about your organization's overall performance: employee engagement, customer satisfaction, and cash flow." Thanks to some great mentors, I used a very similar, narrowed-down focus to identify how to best support a really disengaged team.

Another reason team members are disengaged is that they feel "nobody trained me." If you don't understand their personalities, you may not understand how the team members learn and how to support them best. There are three main types of learning styles—that is, three types of learners:

- **Visual Learners**: Seeing information helps visualize concepts taught.

- **Auditory Learners**: Hearing information helps internalize concepts taught.

- **Kinesthetic Learners**: Using hands or bodies helps experience concepts taught.[4]

Most organizations have some type of training system in place; if you do not, you need to start working on that today, because you will never reach your real potential without training your team. I have seen businesses that refused to put training systems in place have to close their doors after only a few years. They were not willing to ensure the team had the knowledge they needed to meet their client's needs. If you do have a structured training program, team members should have an understanding of what training is available and what expectations they need to meet. If you do not provide them with the tools to be successful, or they don't know what is available, how can you expect them to be engaged, understand their role, and be proficient in their job? If your organization provides training and development opportunities for your team members and they choose not to utilize the tools available, there may be a different issue.

Statistics show that in 2018, US training expenditures were $87.6 billion.[5] Companies are spending massive amounts of money providing tools for their teams, but there are disengaged team members who are not taking advantage of all the resources that are available to them. I've seen time management and stress management classes offered, for which the team members would have been paid to attend, regardless of whether it was offered virtually, or onsite. Team members were not required to attend, but the classes were offered to allow them to receive additional training that would not only help them from a professional standpoint, but also in their personal lives; however, they chose not to attend. This is when understanding different personality styles is important, because with an open line of communication, you are able to understand which obstacles are preventing the team member from feeling supported from a training perspective, and ready to learn what they need to help them become proficient in their role.

I can't even begin to tell you how many times I've heard someone complain about not getting a promotion because they thought they deserved it, or they had been there longer than the person that got the job. Some of it could be because the manager or leader might not have set clear expectations of what was needed for the role, but the primary reasons are due to an entitlement attitude, a lack of understanding of their current performance, or an insufficient proficiency level to advance their career. In this situation, I would recommend having a detailed conversation recapping the interview, or the reasons why the team member did not receive the promotion, then plan a separate time to sit with the associate and explain what your company or organization expects from a performance and proficiency level when looking to hire or promote someone. Here are three steps to recommend to team members interested in moving to a new role:

1. Proficient and Productive in Current Role

2. Expert, and Mentor to Others

3. Identify Next Role and Start Learning

Too often, team members apply for positions when they are not proficient or productive in their current role, or they have not been identified as an expert. However, when the team member is ready for the next position with a clear understanding of what he or she needs to do, it's easy for him or her to grow within the organization.

I'm reminded of a story that my husband, Jay, shared with me about one of his co-workers. It was a hectic day, so Jay asked the coworker if he knew how to run a register. The young man replied, "No." Jay said, "Well, let me teach you." He went on to explain to him that you should always learn as much as you can. The young man replied, "That's not my job. I don't get paid to do that." Because Jay understood how to connect with the young man, he asked him, "Would you rather have a phone that only allows you to call people, or would you rather have a smartphone that can do everything?" Immediately the young man replied, "Well, of course, I want a smartphone!"

Jay went on to explain to the young man that just like he wanted a smartphone, organizations are looking for team members who are engaged, proficient, and productive in their role, and willing to learn and grow. Ultimately, Jay understood the young man's personality and was able to communicate in a way that his teammate would understand, thereby encouraging him to become more engaged.

ABOUT BETH REED-RICHARDSON

Beth Reed-Richardson is a Human Behavior Consultant with Achieve More Growth Company, an organization that helps encourage and inspire individuals and teams so that they can discover their hidden potential. She graduated from Mississippi University for Women where she held leadership roles in civic, social, and government organizations. She also completed the Bloch Strategic Leadership Program at the University of Missouri - Kansas City.

Over the last twenty years, Beth has led winning teams with top performance results while facilitating unparalleled culture within organizations. She is an advocate and volunteer for numerous non-profit organizations in her community. Because growth and development are such an essential part of her life, she became an independent certified Coach, Trainer, and Speaker with The John Maxwell Team, a Certified Human Behavior Consultant affiliated with Personality Insights, and launched the Achieve More Growth Company.

Beth has spent thousands of hours studying the DISC Model of Human Behavior and teaching the model to others. Let her proven track record in leadership development and personal and professional growth be the deciding factor in choosing her to challenge and motivate you and your team. To learn more about working directly with Beth, please connect at:

Website: https://bethreedrichardson.com/

LinkedIn: https://www.linkedin.com/in/bethreedrichardson/

Twitter: https://twitter.com/AskCoachBeth

Instagram: https://www.instagram.com/askcoachbeth/

Chapter Seven

Workplace Culture and Employee Satisfaction

Ron Cooper

Leaders who establish a wholesome, satisfying work environment where people feel they belong frequently have a productive and happy workforce. Leaders who develop a workplace culture of care know that care extends to the family. Work and home are a continuum. If people are happy at work, they frequently arrive home satisfied. Similarly, if the home culture is good, people will often show up for work happy, which leads to productivity in the workplace.

I frequently ask workplace leaders if they have employees or people working for them. Their response can be an early indicator of workplace culture. Having an employee mindset can sometimes indicate a culture where employees are mere timecard punchers. In contrast, leaders with a people mindset want to know the strengths and goals of those in the workforce. People who feel genuinely valued desire to contribute their talents to help advance a company or organization.

Several studies have shown that, across all income levels, the top predictor of workplace satisfaction is the organization's culture and values—*not* pay; the quality of the senior leadership and the career opportunities at the company follow closely behind. Among the six workplace factors Glassdoor examined, compensation and benefits were consistently rated among the *least* important factors of workplace happiness.[1]

Although pay is not the most important driver of employee satisfaction, these results don't suggest that employers can disregard it. Compensation and benefits may have less predictive power for employee satisfaction than the other factors, but it is still the top factor that job seekers consider when evaluating potential employers, according to a recent Glassdoor survey — particularly for job seekers weighing competing offers. To attract talent, offering competitive pay and benefits remains critical for employers.[2]

The Society for Human Resource Management (SHRM) reported that on average, it costs a company six to nine months of an employee's salary to replace him or her. For an employee making $60,000 per year, that comes out to $30,000 - $45,000 in recruiting and training costs.[3]

So, having a wholesome workplace culture (a function of leadership) while having the right person fill a position whose talents match the description, will result in productive people and higher retention rates. Having a DISCiplined (isn't that clever) process can bring these results to the workplace, which will contribute to increased productivity and workplace satisfaction. This helps lead to a high-performing work culture.

My youth, football, and military experience were progressively synergistic in my experiential learning of the importance of relationships to human behavior. As a child, I manifested my personal insecurities, disguised as shyness, by isolating myself from most people. Being raised on a dairy farm and learning that the work is not done until all family members (i.e., the "team") complete their work, you learn the value of working together. We worked together, ate together, and socialized together. This work culture was the onset of a mindset transformation that helped me overcome some of my insecurities, resulting in more effective communication that led to an increased ability to trust people.

The mindset transformation continued to progress through my football experience. Each of the eleven members of a football team must be synchronized in their thinking and execution of each play to function with maximum potential. It was through this experience I learned that mental and physical preparation is integral to trust, and together, they directly affect human behavior. Having a culture of brotherhood in athletics is essential to having a high-performing team.

The importance of a culture of brotherhood and trust was critical as I was able to fulfill a childhood dream of qualifying to become a fighter pilot. I was fortunate to qualify as an F-4 Phantom pilot, and my first operational assignment was to Vietnam. Much of any mission's success is the ability to communicate very effectively while having the discipline to have total situational awareness for every aspect of an intricately planned, fast-paced mission, and for which survival is a function of instantaneously processing a combination of auditory and visual inputs from each member of a high-performing flight team. These three life vignettes were instrumental in helping me overcome my insecurities, which led to a passion for understanding human behavior through personality insights.

What are the components of a high-performing work culture? A high-performing culture is a set of behaviors and norms that lead an organization to achieve superior results by setting clear business goals, defining employees' responsibilities, creating a trusting environment, and encouraging employees to grow continuously and reinvent themselves.

Trust is the preeminent attribute of a high-performing culture, which leads to effective communication within the workplace. Trust is a very personality-dependent attribute that is achieved based on personality style.

I am a D/I personality style blend. My task orientation style frequently leads me to assign a person a "ten" on a ten-point scale for trust, because I listen for conversation content that helps me support that assessment. Some people will prove themselves to be untrustworthy through their actions. I have been burned a few times with that attitude. Therefore, I need people on my team who can temper my judgment/treatment of certain people. I need people around me who are more discerning than I am in some instances.

Empirical evidence tells me that introverted people frequently want more time to develop trust than extroverts. That is one trait of knowing yourself and being comfortable with your limitations. I like to emphasize and grow a person's strengths; I merely acknowledge my and other's weaknesses such that we build a team with complementary attributes.

Developing a high-performing team requires a well-thought-out strategy. This process begins with the team lead knowing themselves. While that might sound a bit trite or elementary to some, it is a primary contributor to self-confidence as the team works toward having complementary skills to advance the company's/organization's goals. Knowing and having confidence in yourself includes knowing your strengths and limitations/vulnerabilities. By knowing yourself, you will know what attributes other members need to provide a complementary skill set to advance the organization's goals.

As a D/I personality style blend, I frequently do not need a calendar or committee to make some decisions: just bring the facts. While that style can work well in some instances, I need people on my team who are good at and enjoy researching facts to ensure I do not make uninformed, hasty decisions.

I have learned that having the right people with talents and personality blends that match the job description results in high-performing work cultures. This process can be used to form new teams, or reform/refine existing teams.

The team building process begins with knowing/defining the group's mission and objectives, so ensure that they are clearly defined. Concurrently, I like to have objective metrics that can be used to help determine if we are meeting those objectives.

With these defined, the job description must be carefully thought out to identify the people we need for the team. The job description is foundational to determining what is to be done in that position, while also describing the attributes required of the person to fulfill the position. Job descriptions frequently overemphasize past experience rather than the personal qualities and values required to be productive in the role. My experience is that having a person with values that align with mine, and with those of the company, is preferable to having a person with more job experience, but whose values do not align with those of the organization. A person possessing the right values along with an insatiable desire to learn can be trained for nearly any position.

With the job descriptions in place, I then determine the personality traits and personal strength attributes of the person who could best fill the position. With these attributes defined, we advertise, possibly through targeted Facebook, LinkedIn, ZipRecruiter, etc., for the type of person needed.

For each person who replies to a position requisition, I administer a DISC personality assessment to ensure they have the personality traits that fit the position to which they are responding. A person might fit better in an area other than the one for which they are applying.

If the person fits the personality profile, we then interview them for the position. Based on the interview, we make a hiring decision based, in part, on whether they will contribute to the culture we are trying to build.

The culture is one of total trust, respect, and confidence. People either have or do not have confidence. The work culture can help strengthen that if someone lacks it coming in. Trust and respect must be given and earned. As a leader, I must earn your trust and respect by first giving it.

The culture I want to build in any organization is one of adding value to people. The "DNA" of an organization must include caring for others. Caring for others includes, but is not limited to, developing a kindred relationship such that we acknowledge and build on each other's strengths while at the same time being aware of our limitations.

How a person thinks is very important to the organization's culture. We can help shape the way a person thinks if they have a teachable spirit. We must DISCern that about each prospective team member.

Once we have the team in place, effective communication becomes paramount. That communication must be congruent (i.e., we know the strategic objective with any conversation topic) and we are always advancing previous conversations. Everyone needs to be accountable for what they say and think. Everyone on the team must be accepting of everyone else's thoughts while also being able to evaluate each other's idea critically to determine its merit whether to advance.

The Team Building Process

This process can work for developing a new team, or re-forming an existing team. For an existing team, the process will determine if the right people are serving in various positions. If the right person is not serving in a certain position, good leaders will strive to find the right placement within a company rather than dismiss the person.

Mission and Objectives: Clearly defining the group's mission and objectives guides the thinking to determine the people needed to fill various positions. If the team being built is in one of the company's divisions, the mission and objectives of the division must support the overall company mission and objectives.

Job Description: The division lead, contract manager, program manager, or project manager would frequently be the person called on to write the job description for each position to be filled. A comprehensive job description is used to recruit the right person to fill each position. If a contract is the determinant of positions to be filled, the Statement of Work would be the source of attributes needed for various positions. If the team is being built or restructured to meet company/division objectives, each position description should be comprehensively written to map to the objectives. The team lead would determine the personality attributes best needed to fill the job.

Personality Assessment: Each person on the team contributes attributes to accomplish the overall objectives. Matching these attributes to the team's objectives will help ensure team harmony. Knowing how to accept each team member's contribution to the team while also knowing how to adapt to another's personality style is paramount to having a high-performing team. The personality type indicator report is the fundamental document to understand human behavior traits.

Interview: Very few people know how to interview effectively. The person conducting the interview needs to determine if the applicant is the right person to fill a position. The interviewer and applicant are obligated to determine if there is a good match of skills and company culture for employment longevity.

- While a low unemployment rate is an indicator of the effectiveness of the local economy, it also means a prospective employee can feel easy turning down a company if the person's expectations do not align with what the company has to offer.

- The interviewee should go into the interview knowing the type of culture that best fits their personality style. The interviewee should "interview" the company by asking open-ended questions to determine how that person or the company would handle various scenarios.

- Similarly, the interviewer wants to learn about a prospective employee's values by asking how they would respond to various situations.

- By creating a very conversational interview environment, stress is reduced, which helps the interviewer become familiar with the interviewee's confidence level. I like to hire people who exhibit a healthy self-confidence.

Teams of all types benefit from this approach through:

- Increased retention, trust, integrity, and proactive conflict resolution

- Worker satisfaction, productivity, and efficiency

- Reduced absenteeism

I have helped several companies and organizations develop high-performing cultures. This begins with leaders whose values are aligned with those of high-performing cultures. These leaders value people and have a passion for helping them achieve their full potential. This is an attitude of intentionality to achieve significance over success. Advancing others is a transformational mindset which is contagious.

ABOUT RON COOPER

Ron Cooper is the Founder and President of The Cooper Culture LLC, a company that partners with entrepreneurs to increase profits and develop high-performing cultures. The Cooper Culture advances organizations by inspiring people to challenge the status quo through quality thinking.

Ron is a twenty-two-year USAF veteran F-4 Phantom pilot and commander who established a reputation for inspiring people to achieve extraordinary results. His leadership acumen and inspirational speaking demeanor are his hallmarks. During his twenty-year corporate career in the aerospace industry, he advanced several organizations from average to high performance, marked by their quality thinking and 90+ percent retention rates. Ron includes critical thinking, human behavior traits, and personal performance coaching to achieve extraordinary personal and organizational results.

Ron ignites people to extraordinary performance through his keynote presentations, seminars, workshops, and consulting. He is noted for his organizational and personal assessments to customize solutions to achieve strategic objectives.

Ron is a DISC Certified Human Behavior Consultant and John Maxwell certified keynote speaker, leadership trainer, and personal performance coach. He transforms organizations by advancing people—one relationship at a time.

To learn more about working directly with Ron, please contact him at:

Website: www.thecooperculture.com

LinkedIn: www.linkedin.com/in/ronaldecooper/

Chapter Eight

From Curious Mom to Passionate Consultant

Karen Bemmes

The DISC Model of Human Behavior is the best marriage, parenting, and life skill tool I've ever learned and used in my life. More than anything, DISC has helped me handle the "difficult" people in my life. Perhaps most importantly, it's helped me understand how *I* might be the difficult person in someone else's life by being unaware of others' priorities.

The first time the DISC system changed my life was nearly twenty years ago, and it was so powerful that I remember it like it was yesterday. I have a sister-in-law I love dearly, but we had a bit of a rocky start. I wanted to be her friend, not just her sister-in-law, so I tried everything I could think of to make that happen. If she was working out in her yard, I would stop and chat with her, but she wouldn't even look up to say hi. One day, I stopped by her house to drop something off, and in the middle of our conversation, her clothes dryer finished its cycle. I was mid-sentence when she turned and walked out of the room without excusing herself. I stood there dumbfounded, expecting her to bring the laundry upstairs to fold while we finished our conversation. She didn't. Eventually, I awkwardly called downstairs to say that I was leaving, and she said goodbye as if it was the most normal thing. I left, convinced I had failed at creating a friendship and that she just didn't like me.

Not long after that, I started reading *Positive Personality Profiles* by Dr. Robert Rohm. While reading before bed one night, I sat straight up, looked at my husband, and told him I understood my sister-in-law for the first time. He laughed and wondered why I cared, but as someone who loves people, what I learned that day changed my life. It took some time to get the courage to ask my sister-in-law about it, but when I did, it was priceless. I told her I had read a book about personalities and asked her if she remembered the day that she left me standing in the kitchen to go downstairs to fold her laundry. She did. I told her that while reading this book, I found out the difference between people who were task-oriented, and people-oriented. So, when she left me standing alone in the kitchen to go downstairs to fold laundry, as a people-oriented person, I thought, "How rude...Doesn't she realize she has a guest?" Through reading *Positive Personality Profiles*, I realized that as a task-oriented person, she was thinking at the same moment, "How rude...Doesn't she see that I have work to do?"

Her face lit up, and her immediate response was, "Exactly!" Then, I told her that I realized when she was working in her yard that my stopping by was a frustrating distraction rather than a welcome one, and she heartily agreed. I knew at that moment that this was some of the most powerful information I'd ever learned, and I could hardly wait to learn more. I also promised that from then on, I would honk and wave rather than stop and chat when I saw her working in the yard. She was thrilled, and we are friends to this day.

One of my favorite lessons from the DISC system was learning how to live harmoniously with my very introverted husband. I am extroverted and love people, which is evidenced by my I/SD personality profile. I tell people that means I want to be determined and driven, but I don't want to hurt anyone's feelings in the process. Instead, I want everyone to enjoy themselves and feel supported in whatever they do. My C/S husband used to say that his dream life was to live on a deserted island surrounded by books. If it weren't for the idea that opposites attract, I'm not sure anyone would understand how we got married, much less stayed happily married for over twenty-five years. What I learned is that when we go to a party, my husband prefers to sit in an out-of-the-way place and people

70

watch. He's happy to talk to anyone who engages him, but he will never "work the room" the way I do. I love to talk to as many people as possible, especially if I know them. I want to hear about what they're doing, how their kids are, where they've traveled, and any good stories they want to tell. I used to think it was my job to drag my husband around the room to interact with people—you know, to bring him out of his shell—but all that did was exhaust both of us. When, thanks to DISC, I learned to understand his introverted nature, I knew he was happier sitting alone than forcing himself to talk with everyone. I quit worrying about whether he was having fun the way I did, and he stopped worrying about pushing himself to be chatty when he didn't feel like it. We both left every party happy rather than exhausted, and it helped our marriage so much to understand that about each other.

It also helps when we are in conflict. When that happens, I need to move and do something to work through the situation. My husband needs to step back and think. Imagine how that played out when I was working, and he was sitting there watching me. It wasn't pretty. I would get angrier by the moment until I finally exploded, and he couldn't understand why. I turned into a martyr, and he withdrew. After learning about DISC, I can honestly count on one hand the number of "fights" we've had. My husband goes somewhere private to think, and I move around as I need to, out of anyone's watchful gaze. It works incredibly well for both of us.

Finally, DISC was invaluable for raising our children. Our oldest son has a very different personality than either my husband or me. From birth, this child was determined and driven. When our son was a toddler, I told my husband that if our son stayed on a positive path, he would be incredibly successful, but if he chose a path of destruction, I wasn't sure we could ever get him back. Luckily for us, DISC came into our lives, and we learned that this child needed challenge and control, and as difficult as it was sometimes, the more we challenged him and let him control his destiny, the better decisions he made. We had to set and uphold boundaries at times, like standing our ground that he was not mature enough to stay out all night with his friends when he was sixteen years old. For the most part, though, we told him that if he took care of his business, we would stay out of it, and it worked. That young man is now married with a fantastic job and a child of his own. He already has plans to further his education and has been promoted twice in two years with the company that hired him out of college. He's still driven, but he has also learned the value of taking care of and paying attention to his family, which puts him way ahead of his parents at the same stage of life.

Our other children are much more like their father. While I could challenge and even criticize my oldest son's actions and he would rise to the challenge, or use the criticism to improve himself, my other two children did not respond to that. Instead, they shut down. For them, criticism, especially from their mother, was devastating. With them, I had to suggest rather than dictate or criticize to keep the lines of communication open. I had to weigh my words more carefully, but knowing that helped me be a better mom to them. Because of that, we celebrated their more methodical approach to life, and it's a delight to see each of them pursue success in their chosen field in their own unique way. Knowing their personality style helps us help them, and appreciate their approach to life. It hasn't always been easy, but as they approach living their independent adult lives, we see that it has definitely been worth it.

For nearly twenty-five years, I was a stay-at-home mom. I used what I learned from DISC everywhere, from being a spouse, to parenting, to dealing with teachers and members of the PTO. DISC helped me appreciate people who are completely different from me, and when my youngest child with extraordinary medical needs and ADHD finally reached adulthood, I decided to officially make DISC part of my return to the workforce, and began looking for certification opportunities. Thankfully, I found Personality Insights and their training program. They confirmed so much of what I had already learned on my own, but they also taught me so much more about how to use that knowledge in every area of life and business. I especially love their positive approach to every personality type when it is in balance, and understanding each personality type when it's out of balance as well.

Now, I work with individuals, families, coaches, and companies that want to improve their careers and their lives using DISC as their guide. At minimum, everyone should take an assessment to understand themselves, and a one-on-one breakdown with a trained consultant is invaluable for insights into how to take what you know and apply it to your real-life issues. The most important thing most people learn is that their natural way of being is a gift, even when they thought it was a curse. I've seen strong women who have been called bad names learn to view their drive and determination as an asset they can celebrate, rather than something they need to defend. I work with coaches whose clients have emailed me after an assessment to tell me they feel understood for the first time in their lives. I've seen people with competing personality traits change before my eyes when I describe their inner conflict without judgment, and give them ways to make peace with that part of themselves.

While I love making money with my new career, seeing that peace and self-acceptance is priceless, and it's what inspires me to share this information with as many people as I can. That way, they can do their jobs better, but more than that, they become better parents, spouses, and human beings as well. Then, when they expand that knowledge by having spouses, family members, and/or co-workers take an assessment, it's as if they see each other for the first time. Just like it was for my sister-in-law and me, their relationship is forever changed for the better. It's why I love what I do and plan to keep doing it for as long as I possibly can.

ABOUT KAREN BEMMES

Karen Bemmes is an author, blogger, DISC consultant, and owner of Moving Toward Better. The mission of Moving Toward Better is to help people live their best life and let the rest go. Using the DISC system, Karen works with women entrepreneurs and couples to help them understand themselves and appreciate others. She helps individuals see their hidden talents, and couples appreciate their partners' qualities, particularly the ones that are different and complementary to their own. Karen also helps other mothers understand their unique personality style and use that knowledge to enhance their parenting, as well as marital and professional relationships.

While Karen chose to turn her appreciation of the DISC principles into a career after her children grew up, she used the principles to parent her children, and appreciate the talents of teachers, coaches, PTA members, and more.

Through keynote presentations, workshops, books, and one-on-one consulting, Karen teaches people to use their own personality traits to interact more effectively with their co-workers, partners, and family members to create an equally fulfilling professional and personal life.

To connect with Karen, visit:

Website: www.movingtowardbetter.com

Email: whatsup@movingtowardbetter.com

Facebook: https://www.facebook.com/movingtowardbetter/

Instagram: https://www.instagram.com/movingtowardbetter/

LinkedIn: https://www.linkedin.com/in/karen-bemmes-2787459/

Chapter Nine

Sales Is a Competitive Sport!

Susan Davis

You just gave the best sales presentation of your life, or so you thought. You provided every feature, turned it into a benefit, answered objections with confidence, and closed the sale, only to hear the word NO! The potential customer tells you, "We aren't sure; we need to think a little bit more on this," but you know that they need your service or product. You are passionate about the solutions that you offered and just knew that they would accept your proposal. Feeling defeated, you pick up your files, gather your belongings, and head toward the door. You know you will have some explaining to do to your boss.

Sales is a competitive sport, and it often feels like no playbook or instruction manual comes with it. Just like athletes, sales professionals need ongoing coaching, training, skill development, and strategy. Do you think a National College Championship team or professional Super Bowl team plays the same way against each team? Does Mia Hamm, professional soccer player and two-time Olympic gold medalist, use the same strategies for each game? No! They adapt their playing, their approach, their defense, and their offense to their competitor. If they played the same way against each team, they would not be successful.

Successful athletes and sales professionals always look for ways to improve their level of play. You must continually practice and develop new skills, but you also must adapt yourself to stay ahead and, more importantly, to deliver value to your customer and close the deal. Tiger Woods, professional PGA and Master's winner once said, "No matter how good you get, you can always get better. That's the exciting part." Never stop developing yourself to get better.

As with a professional athlete, it is the job of a salesperson to practice, work out, and hone skills. Salespeople do so many things correctly, but there is also a complacency that can overtake them. Salespeople can easily feel overconfident, relying on their "sales skills," outgoing personalities, talkative nature, tenure in the business, and ability to think on their feet to close a deal. Be honest...Have you ever said to yourself: "I am a good salesperson, I don't need to rehearse. I've been doing this for ten plus years; I don't need to practice handling objections. I can do this in my sleep."? I hope you answered truthfully, because we have all been there. I was always told that I was a "natural" salesperson. I have an outgoing personality; I can speak extemporaneously, and can make people feel comfortable. I always felt like I could rely on my ability to think on my feet to close that sale, that is, until I started learning the science of sales and how I could become more effective by developing my skills as a sales professional. Of those learned skills, I have found that the ones most beneficial to my career are the ability to understand my own communication and personality style, as well that of being able to recognize and adapt to my customers' various personality, communication, and buying styles.

I had my first sales training exposure to the DISC assessment when I went through new hire training with Pfizer Pharmaceuticals over seventeen years ago. I already thought I was a decent salesperson. I knew my products as well as my competitors, and I thought I had those "natural" sales skills; at least that is what I had always been told. I recall attending my first two weeks of training in Reston, Virginia, and thinking to myself, *I know the products; I am learning my competitors—I've got this*! The next two weeks were spent in New York, and this is where the real sales training began. We all took the DISC assessment and were informed of our personality and communication style, but it didn't end there. Over the next two weeks, we had to deliver sales presentations based upon the different personality and communication styles. We would walk up to an instructor, they would flip their badge, and on the spot, we had to deliver a sales presentation based upon their personality style. *Wow*, this just got a lot more interesting! We had to do this over fifty times and were also videotaped during many presentations so we could evaluate our sales presentations. I can honestly say, this was the most long-term, impactful training that I have participated in over my eighteen years in formal sales roles. I started "DISCing" everyone I came into contact with—friends, family, current and future customers. I could walk into an office, sit down, look around at the walls and desk and, without even speaking to the customer, I could almost with certainty tell you what their personality style was. This is a skill I not only developed, but practiced over and over, and it gave me a competitive advantage over my competition because I did not waste valuable meeting time trying to figure out how to sell to them. It took the sales relationship to a new level with the customer—one which my competitors did not have.

Salespeople face many challenges; chief among them are: pressure to meet quotas, to close deals, and to build long-term relationships with potential customers. When pressure increases, a salesperson becomes more uncomfortable dealing with customers who have a different personal style than their own. They revert to their tried and true sales strategies and tactics of pushing hard, and quite often, they are unable to modify their behavior to meet the needs of their customers, hence the sale is lost. The seller and buyer each have unique personality styles, and most often they are entirely different. What happens when the decision-maker has a different personality style than the salesperson? If all of your clients were precisely alike, sales would be much easier, but that's not the case. If each customer you came into contact with made decisions the same way, communicated the same way, and bought the same way, you would be sitting in President's Club year after year. The reality is that your job is dependent on the behavior of your customers, and this varies from person to person.

Your ability to influence your customer's behavior is the key to your sales success. If you are not able to affect your customer positively, you will cripple your closing rate. The challenge is that all of your customers have different personalities that will likely be different than yours. Imagine that the world consists of four groups of people, and each group speaks a unique language. What happens if you're responsible for communicating with each group, but you only speak one of the languages? How will you communicate with the 75 percent who speak a different language? "If I only speak one language, I'm only going to make one sale out of every four," Kelly explained. "But if I speak all four languages, I'll sell four out of four." It's precisely why a study of DISC profiling is a must for every salesperson."[1]

Personality Insights uses validated studies in assessing the global community. According to the studies, we know that roughly 30 percent of the population are considered I, 35 percent are considered S, 25 percent are considered C, and 10 percent are considered D.[2] To be successful in sales, you must get out of your comfort zone, change your strategy, learn new skills, and practice those skills. The good news is, you can! If you are looking for a competitive edge, an advantage—incorporate DISC into your selling skills. This will enable you to improve your level of play. It is crucial for professional and personal growth, as well as in terms of increasing your win rate, closing more deals, and becoming a sales professional that is considered a valuable team member to the customer. DISC profiles will help you understand the 75 percent of customers who are not like you.

Let me explain DISC quickly, and then I can show you how it can increase your sales and win rates too. The DISC model is based upon our natural tendencies: the way we behave and think. It helps us understand behavior, temperament, and personality. William Marston first described the foundation of DISC in his 1928 book, *Emotions of Normal People.* Marston identified what he called four "primary emotions" and associated behavioral responses which we know today as D (Dominance - how you handle problems), I (Influence - how you influence people), S (Steadiness - the pace at which you do things) and C (Conscientiousness - attention to detail or willingness to follow rules). It helps us understand why people behave, act, and think the way they do. Once you know the personality, communication, and buying style of your customers and then adapt your style to fit theirs, you will find it to be a potent sales tool that will give you a competitive advantage. I do not see it often used in the field when I do sales calls or field rides, but when I do, I see successful sales professionals that have a better and more powerful relationship with their customers. It is a powerful tool when implemented, practiced, and consistently used.

Before delivering a sales presentation or making a sales call, you must understand not only your basic personality and selling style, but also that of your audience. Who will you be presenting to? Do you know their basic personality or communication style? Salespeople go through training to understand how to prospect, qualify a lead, manage a strategic deal, and close opportunities, but rarely do they adjust their communication or presentation style to fit the needs of their customers. One way to develop further skills that will enable growth is by adopting the DISC method of communication and selling. Have you ever taken any type of personality assessment? Your company may have had everyone take an assessment, explained that you were either a D, I, S, or C and then moved on to the next flavor of the month in sales training. An assessment has little to no meaning unless it is explained, applied, and adapted, and it is also something that should be continually reinforced and re-trained, because just knowing your personality and communication style is only the tip of the iceberg. DISC can help you to connect with your customers, understand their exact needs, and deliver quality solutions. When you know how to recognize different customers' personality types, offer products or services in a way that meets the customer's needs, and can provide solutions to the customer's problems, it strengthens relationships and your brand. For example, how you approach a sales call for an Influencer personality type may be completely different than how you would sell to someone with a Steadiness personality type. When you don't understand how to speak to and communicate with each customer/personality type in a persuasive and meaningful way, the buying window will close quickly, and most times in sales, you don't get a second chance to make a first impression.

There are several things that you need to understand about communicating and selling to your current and potential customers:

1. Understand that everyone talks and receives information differently.

2. Know your own personality and communication style. It will enable you to understand your selling style.

3. Identify and understand the communication and personality style of your customer. It will also enable you to comprehend their buying style.

4. Understand that everyone is a unique blend of several styles.

5. Adjust YOUR style to fit that of your customer to increase sales and win rates.

6. Avoid assumptions based on personality styles.

7. Understand your least comfortable style and practice! Don't go in cold with a potential customer, especially when their style is the one you are least comfortable with.

8. Understand that not everyone makes buying decisions the same way you do.

9. Avoid putting your own sales style on "autopilot."

10. Practice, rehearse, practice, rehearse, and practice some more!

Once you understand your personality and communication style, you can essentially speak any customer's language; the upshot is that they leave the conversation feeling good about you, *and* your product or service.

Because everyone is a unique blend of personality styles, being able to identify critical characteristics in your customers is essential for sales success. Once you start intentionally recognizing and gauging in DISC, it will become automatic to you in the sales process. Understanding and applying the principles of DISC is an additional way for you to increase your sales skills proficiency, but do not forget that you must practice keeping these skills sharp. Also, remember that DISC is not just about assessing your potential customer at the beginning of the sale. Implement DISC throughout the entire sales process, from the initial meeting to the final close and delivery of products or services. Always be aware of your DISC style and personality, but be even more aware of your customers' styles. Always adapt your style to theirs and carry it through, enabling you to be seen not only as a sales professional, but also as a valued member of their team, providing solutions to their needs.

Sales is a competitive sport. To win the championship and achieve gold, you need to continually coach yourself, develop new skills, change strategies, and practice consistently. As the legendary coach John Wooden said, "Winning takes talent. To repeat takes character."

ABOUT SUSAN DAVIS

Susan H. Davis is the Director, Global Sales Training for the PSG Division of Thermo Fisher Scientific and also the Founder and President of S.H. Davis Empowerment Group.

Susan is a seasoned sales, training, and leadership professional with over eighteen years' experience in the medical, pharmaceutical, and nonprofit industry. Susan is known for her high-energy style, coupled with her extreme passion for working with people and teams to empower them to abandon mediocrity, set goals, and deliver exceptional value to their customers with intentionality.

Susan has helped companies set goals that break current boundaries. Susan shares this message through training, coaching, and keynote speaking and has worked with clients from a variety of backgrounds, including corporate groups, schools, real estate, medical sales, and nonprofit groups. Susan's style is collaborative and results-driven.

With a bachelor's and master's degree, Susan is also a Certified Advanced DISC Facilitator, Certified Facilitator for Professional DynaMetrics Programs (PDP), Certified Facilitator for Executive

Presentations Skills and Socratic Selling for Communispond, and a John Maxwell Team Certified Leadership Trainer, Speaker, and Coach.

To learn more about working directly with Susan, please connect at:

Website: www.shdavisempowerment.com

Email: shdavisempowerment@gmail.com

LinkedIn: https://www.linkedin.com/in/susanhdavis/

John Maxwell Team Site:
https://www.johncmaxwellgroup.com/susandavis

Chapter Ten

Coaching High-Performance Teams: Flexing Your DISC Style

Matthew Clark

The Coach's Tool Box

Coaching high-performance teams is a delicate balance of art and science. Success doesn't happen just because you show up—it takes a well-thought-out plan, and the tenacity to push through performance barriers. Teams consist of people, and as a coach, you will need to learn how to navigate their personalities. However, there is one tool that helps remove the guesswork out of understanding human behavior, and it should be in every leader's toolbox. The DISC Model of Human Behavior has proven to be highly effective at illuminating and defining personality types and behavioral tendencies. Understanding the different personality of each team member and how it affects team dynamics is fundamental to the success of your team. Are you sometimes puzzled at why people behave and respond the way they do in certain situations? Why doesn't everyone act the same way? The answer to those questions and many more became clear to me when I received an MRI (massive revolutionary insight) to my personality through DISC assessments and certification. The DISC Model of Human Behavior has given me a rich understanding of the four basic temperaments and the four personality styles associated with human behavior. As a result, I continue to gain greater self-awareness, and my improved ability to understand and connect with others has positively impacted my executive coaching and consulting.

I had the privilege of spending sixteen seasons coaching pit crews for Jeff Gordon, Jimmie Johnson, and other NASCAR® Championship drivers. I was responsible for recruiting, building up, and coaching individuals who were able to handle the pressure and stress of winning races and championships. On pit road, success is measured by tenths, and sometimes hundredths of a second. Pit crews perform five to eight pit stops per race, which equates to approximately ninety seconds of work. Each time the car hits pit road for tires and fuel, the crew member's job hangs in the balance, and the performance of the entire organization is on the line. Race day success is leveraged to secure precious sponsorship dollars that fund team budgets. Every finishing position gained adds to the bottom line. Performance determines longevity in the sport.

The Pit Stop

What happens during a pit stop is a microcosm of a thriving workplace, and it applies to any team. Everyone has a specific role, and hopefully, leadership has set performance goals, KPIs, and defined wins and losses for the team. In any endeavor, the red-hot furnace of performance exposes the imperfections and gaps in preparation while also magnifying failures in execution. However, success always starts with YOU! Self-awareness is the first step to increasing performance in any field. Understanding your DISC personality style, or how you are "wired," will help you become more successful in all areas of your personal and professional life.

DISC in Action

When presenting "The 5 Lug Nuts of a High-Performing Team," I begin with Lug Nut #1, the foundational precept: *Know Yourself, Know Your Team.* Successful coaches understand the culture of their team, and that falls more into the art of coaching. DISC adds some science to the mix and drills down to the individual level, giving insights as to how personality style can contribute to the overall success of the team. If you want to understand your team better, start with learning the DISC personality style of the individuals that make up your team. A competent coach can connect to, communicate with, motivate, and inspire all four basic DISC personality styles.

Flex Your Style

Depending on the situation, you may have to flex your approach to a style that might not be as comfortable for you. Flexing is merely transitioning to your less dominant behavior (those that fall well below the midline on your DISC graph) to generally mirror the style of the person you're communicating with. For example, I register Very Low C style on my DISC graph; I struggle with the details. I'm a big picture guy, fast-paced, and I like flexibility. Therefore, when I'm dealing with a Cautious style in certain situations, I have to slow my roll, focus more on the details, and have a systematic plan. Trust me: it's difficult for me to do because it is out of my comfort zone. Flexing your style will take keen awareness and authenticity to truly master. However, when you do, positive results will follow.

When a coach tries to connect with a team member using only their own personality style, it can be frustrating for everyone. Each person has a unique personality blend and style. When a coach flexes his or her own style, communication is more effective. Many coaches fail to connect, and often lose their team when they coach everyone the same way. We are all blends of the four basic personality styles, and as such, we require different approaches at different times. Understandably, there has to be uniformity and consistency of the messaging by the coach. We all have a natural personality style that makes us unique.

As a communications major, the first communication axiom I learned was "know your audience." During my sixteen seasons dealing with high-performance athletes and teams, I learned the value of coaching to the individual. What works for some will not work with others. If performance matters in the slightest, there has to be a plan to get there. A basic understanding of the four personality styles, and how those styles blend in differing amounts within each of your team members is a primary key to success. It's up to you to do the work to figure out how to unlock performance in your team. The following insights will help you better understand how to approach each personality style. Let's open the toolbox.

The Dominant Style

As a High D, I like it when coaches speak in a sharp, direct, and challenging manner. When I fail, my first thought is that I let myself down; I'm frustrated that I didn't maximize the opportunity—that kind of thinking illustrates the D personality. You can talk more directly to, and use stronger tones with the D style personality. They embrace the challenge and might even push back when you "get in their business." Coaches can speak with tones and directness that will move them in a positive direction; however, other personality styles might find the same conversation abrasive, or even rude. The High Ds are looking for feedback so they can fix what went wrong immediately. You can tell a D style person very directly what you observed, and sometimes, in a loud and animated way, they will tell you what "actually" happened. These conversations will put most others on edge because they are direct, passionate, and sometimes downright confrontational. Don't let it bother you if your style is different...Flex to the D style when communicating with a D style personality. However, you better hang on because they like lively verbal sparring. On the positive side, the Ds will not hold a grudge: being direct is how we want to communicate. In our minds, it's over, so move on and get back to winning!

The Influencing Style

"I" personality types love people *and* a party! What does an I personality style do after busting off a great pit stop? You guessed it! They celebrate, jump around, and give high fives to everyone on the team. Success for them is just another invitation to celebrate. I styles make it fun to win, no doubt about it. However, when dealing with failure or mistakes, they can be challenging at times. The people who crack jokes at the most inappropriate times, and make light of "serious" situations are most likely the I style. When coaching these folks, use a more lighthearted approach when possible. Sarcasm and a little joking will keep the atmosphere light. If you get too intense for too long, you are bound to lose them. Help them refocus and get back on track by keeping your communication upbeat, positive, and about the team. The I style also needs time to bounce back once the wind has gone out of the out of their sails. Remind them that there is always something to celebrate! It's 4:59 somewhere!

The Supportive Style

Coaching the Supportive personality style takes finesse and a high EQ (emotional quotient). Sensitivity and word choice are paramount to maximizing performance. The tones and methods that worked for the D and I styles will not be effective with the S style. For the Supportive style, it's all about keeping your tone in check and maintaining peace and harmony. Providing an atmosphere of comradery and teamwork best suits this style. The conversations become "you and I are in this together" rather than "me versus you." When an S fails, they carry the weight of letting the entire team down. As a result of that feeling, they tend to take on more than they can handle to make sure it doesn't happen again. When they try to do too much, it can wreak havoc on performance. While making sure that everyone else is taken care of, the S style can neglect their own core responsibilities. When letdowns happen, allow these individuals to prioritize the tasks that will positively impact outcomes. Warmly remind them that they are a valuable member of the team, because they want to feel valued and included. The S style will need even more time than the D or I style to put all the pieces back together after a failure. When giving feedback, let them process the situation; don't rush it—there is already a feeling that they let everyone down due to their poor performance. Follow up with an action plan that will move them in the right direction. If you are not a Supportive style blend, flexing to this style will take work and deliberate practice to master. However, once you connect, rest assured, the S will be loyal to a fault.

The Cautious Style

Ever get a blank stare after an emotional, passionate speech? Well, you've most likely locked eyes with a C style. These folks make you wonder if you are even speaking the same language. They generally have a more monotone, non-emotional, analytical approach to life. When coaching the Cautious style, use facts, figures, and relevant information, along with a very systematic approach. Details matter immensely to the C style, so include as many as possible in the action plan. Work on a step-by-step plan that will generate the desired outcome. The Cs are not outwardly emotional. Coaches love to connect with the heart; however, to communicate with a C style, you have to speak to the mind. The Cs think, rather than feel. The D style approach will do more harm than good when coaching an S or a C style. Keep your tone and pace in check, or risk an immediate communication shutdown. A useful exercise to consider is to have them walk you through the performance step-by-step in vivid detail. Let *them* explain what happened and why they think it happened. It's a cathartic analysis of sorts, and it will bring them full circle. Now, you have your coaching opportunity. Make it count...It's what you live for as a coach.

The Checkered Flag

It takes work to understand yourself, and even more work to understand others. Flexing to different styles takes practice. While it may come easier to some, no one becomes great without effort. It is vitally important to the success and longevity of your coaching relationships that you learn to communicate to your team members on the level that is most effective to them. Long-term, it builds more in-depth relationships, engenders trust, and allows you to become more open and transparent. When there is a mutual understanding of the different personality styles on the team, communication, trust, and performance will increase.

As a former championship pit crew coach and current consultant, executive coach, and speaker, I understand the value of team dynamics, human behavior, and the impact it has on production, both in the athletic and business world. It is the understanding and application of the DISC methodology that will increase the performance of your team. These principles universally apply to all relationships. On a personal level, I am now more aware of my behavioral tendencies, and both the positive and negative effects my actions have on others. I can share some not-so-proud coaching moments, when I've smashed stopwatches, yelled, and screamed like an out-of-control High D personality type...Not very proud, for sure! However, understanding the DISC model of human behavior has given me more profound insights into myself and others. I've learned to predict my behavior, navigate it, and communicate more effectively. DISC has not only made me a better coach, but more importantly, it has helped me be a better husband, father, and person.

ABOUT MATTHEW CLARK

Matt is a championship pit crew coach who has a unique perspective on high-performance team building and coaching. During his sixteen seasons, he was part of five NASCAR® Championships, and over eighty race wins. He also covered the sport as an on-air analyst for Fox Sports1®.

Matt's career includes wins at the five most prestigious races on the circuit: The Daytona 500 (biggest), The EA Sports 500 (fastest), The Brickyard 400 (richest), The Mountain Dew® Southern 500 (oldest), and The Coca Cola® 600 (longest). His teams garnered multiple awards, including the Checkers®/Rally's® Double Drive-Thru Challenge, Mechanix Wear ®Most Valuable Pit Crew, and the Craftsmen® Pit Crew Challenge Championship®.

Matt has leveraged his experience to positively impact executives and organizations by adding value through coaching, training, workshops, and keynotes that focus on DISC methodology, leadership development, and team building. He understands the challenges of developing leaders, building teams, and achieving results in an extremely competitive environment.

Using a P.I.T. (Powerful, Intentional, Transformation) approach, he works with executives and organizations to improve culture, communication, and leadership effectiveness. To learn more about how Matt Clark can impact your organization or event, connect with him at:

Website: http://mattclarkmc.com/

LinkedIn: https://www.linkedin.com/in/mattclarkmc/

Twitter: https://twitter.com/MattClarkMC

Chapter Eleven

Going from Information to Transformation

Cherie Dasmacci

My journey with personality and behavior styles has evolved a lot over the last several years. My first experience with DISC was when I went to work for a real estate company back in 2004. They would do an assessment before hiring anybody to make sure they were best suited for the role for which they were applying. Some styles were better suited for customer service, others were better for accounting or management, while still others were a fit for sales. It was very informative to learn about my behavior style. I am a High D/I. Some traits I was already aware of, and it explained why I was so drawn to an independent, entrepreneurial lifestyle. Other characteristics were less than flattering, but showed how I might sometimes come across too strong and intimidate others. It was valuable insight, but I was not taught how to use this information while interacting with others. At the time, I didn't realize that was important. When I entered the coaching program as an agent, they did give us examples of how to adapt our presentation to certain types of people. They usually used their career as an example. For instance, when dealing with an engineer or an accountant (which I later learned were primarily C types), we should get straight to the point and be accurate with numbers and statistics, not waste time with the fluff of personal conversation and asking about family, etc. While that was helpful, that was a very narrow segment of the clientele that I would deal with. A few years later, when they offered me a leadership position with the company, they put me through their internal training on how to administer assessments to people I was considering hiring. Once again, the point was to make sure I was putting people in a proper role. While the report did notate suggestions on how to manage the individual, and mentioned the type of environment that motivates them, it did not go into a whole lot of detail on how to best interact with them on a daily basis. After reviewing several of these assessments and learning about the other behavior styles that were different from my own, I started to figure out that many of us perceive things very differently. No one is more right or wrong than another, but each has unique perspectives. I also learned that many of us are motivated differently...For instance, some people are motivated by money, some people crave recognition from their superiors or their peers, while others just want security and stability. The ways we communicate also vary. Some people needed specific details on the plan and the reasons why they were doing something, while others could just take an idea and run with it. I realized where some breakdowns in communication were happening, and why I was scratching my head trying to figure out why some people just couldn't seem to understand what I was trying to get them to accomplish. I was communicating with people in my style's language, and when I trained them on how to do their job, I would teach them in the same way I would do it. While that worked for some, it left others looking like deer in the headlights. They were lost, confused, or sometimes just plain intimidated. It wasn't until I dug deeper that I realized it wasn't a problem with them, it was a problem with the way I was interacting with them. This light bulb moment has since helped me both professionally and personally. The more I realized how my communication style was affecting the people I worked with, I began reflecting back and seeing how these same miscommunications had impacted some of my personal relationships. That is when I decided to pursue more advanced training, and started sharing this knowledge with others. If learning to adapt my communication style could help me with my group of agents and clients, imagine what it could do on a larger scale! I know of so many companies with challenges in production, as well as employee retention. What if I could share this valuable information with the leaders of those companies? What kind of positive impact could it have on their organization?

Imagine working with a large organization that is very strong on research and statistics to help keep them the leader in the marketplace. They consistently measure their success with numbers and graphs, and communicate with everybody on the team in that same manner: with numbers and stats. While that works for many of them, some people need a different approach. Now don't get me wrong: companies are after a profit, and the numbers are extremely important. The company's goals, however, are achieved by people, who are simply a diverse group of individuals with their own thoughts, feelings, and needs. All the team members bring their unique talents and strengths to the project. In situations like I just described, many of the employees start feeling like nothing more than a number on a spreadsheet rather than feeling valued as people, and for what they contribute to the company. This most often leads to low morale, decreased production, and high turnover of team members. To succeed, leaders need to engage their team and get them to all understand and buy into the goal. When the team is on the same page and motivated, amazing things can take place.

Let me back up for just a minute and elaborate on some of my own discoveries. As I mentioned earlier, I am a High D/I. I tend to float back and forth between those styles fairly equally, with Very Low S and C lingering in the background. When I am operating in my "Driver" mode, I do not like to be bogged down with too many details, and I do not have the patience for small talk. If the person attempting to communicate with me does either of those things, my natural response is to tune them out. My brain goes back to thinking of what needs to get done and how I can exit the conversation so I can get back to doing them; therefore, their message is lost on me. However, in my "Inspiring" mode, I am ready to network and socialize. I can become a bit of a chatterbox, and if the person isn't showing any interest in what I have to say, I may get bored and move on to someone who will engage. Now, if I am adversely affected by how others communicate with me, I wondered how often I have caused others to shut down by how I communicate with them. I have heard others use their style as an excuse for their behavior and expect others to adapt to them. But if we genuinely want to be successful, we need to take it upon ourselves to adapt to those we are trying to serve. After all, we now know better, right? Those of us who have been enlightened with this powerful information need to take responsibility to use it for the greater good.

None of us can change how our communication styles are wired, but once we are aware of our strengths, as well as areas we can improve upon, we can make a conscious effort to modify our approach when dealing with those who have different styles. It's amazing how changing a few words, or even the pace of your speech, can make a difference in whether or not you connect with someone. I began with small changes. For instance, I send out a lot of emails in my line of work. When I am operating in my D mode, I often come across as abrupt, or even cold. Remember, in the written word, tone and inflection is up to the interpretation of the reader—which is not always what the sender intended. While multitasking, I might send a direct, to-the-point message with no real opening or ending. So, I began to pause before hitting "send" in order to consider my recipient. Now, I often add a warmer greeting (for example, "Aloha, I hope you are doing well") before jumping straight to the nitty-gritty; I may also alter the sign off with something personal, or perhaps the next step in our plan. On the flip side, if I am in my I mode, I might write more casually, add too much explanation or social commentary, and even unnecessary emojis—which would be fine for another I personality style, but again, I need to consider my recipient, and I will often cut the length of my message down. If I sent that email as is to another D, they probably wouldn't even read beyond the first sentence or two. Now, what about when I am sending a message to my whole team? I've learned to accommodate their diverse styles. I open by addressing all the people first, with the bottom line of the objective for next, and then elaborate in more detail for those who need it. Those who only wanted the basic concept can move on, and those who want the how and the why can keep reading. I realize this is not some amazing new concept that will suddenly change your life, but it is a step in the right direction, and it *will* improve your interactions with others. The goal is to practice these techniques and gradually implement these changes in the way you communicate in all areas— one-on-one meetings, sales presentations, and even conversations with your loved ones. It will eventually become second nature.

Let's get back to how this applies to leadership in a large organization. We've all heard the saying, "People don't quit jobs, they quit bosses." If a leader isn't making an effort to connect with their employees, the employees will not feel valued. If employees do not feel valued, it affects their productivity, and certainly their loyalty. I do not believe bosses—for the most part—are intentionally mean or dismissive. Many just don't have the knowledge and the tools to reach their potential and inspire their team to reach theirs. But they all have the ability to acquire it if they choose. That is where I, and other Certified Human Behavior Consultants, come in.

The process begins with an assessment, but the transformation comes with the training on how to use the information on a daily basis to improve your communications with others, professionally and personally, to achieve better results. When we work with teams and utilize some interactive exercises to help them gain a better understanding of their peers, relationships are improved and productivity increases. Change always needs to begin at the top. If the leader is willing to become educated and make adjustments to how he or she leads and interacts with team members in *their* language, team members will begin to feel valued and understood, and it becomes a domino effect within the organization. That is why it is imperative to involve the whole team, not just the leaders. Get everyone on board and make it part of the company culture. The leaders in the company I referred to earlier had no clue they were alienating half the team by always speaking in facts and figures. They were struggling with high turnover, and couldn't pinpoint the reason. Once that realization was brought to the forefront and they were armed with the tools to engage everyone, the environment became much more cohesive. It didn't take a lot of effort for the leaders to reach out to those with different styles and speak to them in a way they felt understood and valued. Because this was a cultural shift being promoted within the organization, the objectives were transparent, and the whole team bought into the process. Once they knew that the leadership was making a conscious effort to better connect, they made more of an effort with each other. They also felt more comfortable speaking up to leadership when they had a question or challenge because it now felt safe whereas it did not before.

I have barely scratched the surface on how understanding DISC has made a positive impact on my life, my business, and my clients. I know of marriages that have been saved, parent-child relationships that have improved, and companies that have flourished by not only understanding their own behavior style and the styles of others, but learning how to integrate that knowledge into their everyday interactions. I still continue to learn and grow through this process. With every new client and each new business opportunity, I gain deeper knowledge. This is not a one-and-done solution—this is a choice in mindset and knowledge that should be continuously practiced. Are you ready to start achieving your team's true potential? If so, then understand that taking an assessment is only the first step. Creating a culture of high performance involves establishing a culture that thrives on properly understanding and utilizing the strengths of all the communication styles found throughout the entire team. I can help. Let's create something incredible!

ABOUT CHERIE DASMACCI

Cherie is a Coach, Speaker, Trainer and Real Estate Broker located on the island of Maui in Hawaii.

Cherie has extensive business development experience in both the corporate world and as a business owner. Throughout her career and her personal life, she has experienced success, and faced adversity. Every situation we face in life contains a lesson, and there are rewards and consequences for each choice we make. With the right tools, we can make better decisions and have enhanced productivity, personal growth, and a better life.

Cherie intentionally surrounds herself with goal-oriented people who share her values. They have helped her grow into the person she is today, and continue to help her be a better person tomorrow. She is passionate about helping others achieve their goals. She is a certified Coach with the John Maxwell Team and a Certified Human Behavior Consultant with Personality Insights. Through her company, Aspire Leadership Development, she works with individuals, teams, and leadership to help them improve communication, increase productivity, and impact results. She offers workshops, seminars, mastermind groups, and keynote speaking, as well as individual coaching. She customizes training programs to serve the needs of your organization. To learn more about working with Cherie, please visit www.AspireLeadershipDevelopment.com.

Chapter Twelve

The DISC Mirror: A Reflection Tool for Fully Knowing Yourself and Others

Ana Berdecía

As water reflects the face, so one's life reflects the heart.[1]

Have you ever looked in the mirror and forgotten what you've seen, only to go back and look again? Have you ever been curious as to how you "show up" for life—either full of confidence and assurance, or plagued by limiting beliefs and doubts? Or perhaps you've been curious as to how others see you? The DISC Model of Human Behavior provides business people and leaders with an excellent tool for fully knowing who we are, and how we show up for life. It helps us understand not only how we are naturally wired, but also reveals our pace in life, allowing us to truly see ourselves, as well as the way in which others see us.

When we first look at our DISC report, it is like looking into a mirror, but we soon forget what we have read. The second look in the mirror involves partnering with a trained eye—a coach that can create an experience that helps us unpack the meaning behind the descriptors and the statements about oneself in a way that reconfirms, validates, and reinforces strengths, and possible blind spots. That second look in the mirror allows each of us to be transformed from the inside out. It is never enough just to take an assessment and be done with it...The true gift is found in the study of our own personality type, digging deeper into the essence of our human nature, and deciding how we can be even better people and leaders. Developing new lenses through which you see both yourself and others is a skill that every leader needs.

John C. Maxwell writes, "No one can become a good leader without making efforts to understand other people."[2] The DISC Model of Human Behavior is a powerful tool in the hands of leaders because it allows them to begin the process of honest self-reflection and self-discovery. Gabrielle Bernstein states, "The way we experience the world around us is a direct reflection of the world within us."[3] I believe that the DISC personality profile provides an extraordinary examination of our "public self" and our "private self" situationally. It shows how comfortable we are in our own skin, and how others might perceive us as we interact with them. In addition, the DISC personality profile helps people view their strengths as part of a team, and how they perform in stressful situations and environments.

It takes courage to hold up the DISC mirror to ourselves and not forget what we see, but rather remember our strengths, talents, and abilities. It helps us to recognize our brilliance, as well as our blind spots. In doing so, we can start to make adjustments in our behaviors, so at the end of the day we can say, "We did our best to be authentic and connect with the people in our lives in meaningful ways."

As a bilingual Latina woman who is a life/leadership coach and trainer, I work in urban cities in the Northeast United States with nonprofits, school-based organizations, ministry organizations, and other captains of industry. I work with C-Suite, senior and junior executives in organizations of 20 to 600 employees. My clients are primarily women, entrepreneurs, and ministry leaders. I have used the DISC assessment as a reflective tool that provides leaders with a glimpse of who they are, and with opportunities to make subtle or major adjustments to improve their confidence, as well as their interactions with the people closest to them. When I administer DISC assessments and seminars to executives and teams, they gain an appreciation of the people around them and new lenses through which to see their teams, co-workers, family members, and their world. I thoroughly enjoy working with teams to enhance communication, increase employee engagement, and raise productivity. Through personal growth, team building, and leadership development seminars, I have helped professionals examine human behaviors and personality types that make their workforce unique, and have helped them adopt strategies to create an understanding of diverse points of view, which in turn, improves their business communications exponentially.

My unique DISC personality blend is DCIS, but I often show up as a D/C. The DISC report heightened my awareness of how people perceive me, and that awareness made me want to "show up" differently. I had to understand that being a D/C—a double task-oriented leader— was a unique personality blend that makes the world a better place, and that my blind spots could be improved with greater awareness of them. I had to create my own narrative to embrace the "Drive" in me, and own up to the fact that being too demanding could alienate the very people I desire to work with on a daily basis. I also had to accept that my C traits showed up daily too in my love for data, creativity, solutions, and options.

When using the profile with my clients, I often encourage them to circle the descriptors on their DISC report that resonate most with them, and strike the traits that do not. I also encourage them to place a question mark on the descriptors that they need to unpack further as they consider the frequency with which the descriptors show up in their interactions with other people. As a fellow coach once said, "You know yourself better than anyone." This process allows my clients to feel validation for who they are, and not feel like they have to be something they are not, or that they have to show up like someone they are not.

Through coaching, my clients maximize their strengths and make adjustments for their blind spots. Together, we can unpack their behaviors and gain greater clarity as to how they show up for life. One example of this is when I shared my blind spots with another executive. She quickly admitted that she does the same thing, and it made her aware of how others might perceive her. It is very beneficial to understand personality types and how each is fueled: this is what makes people thrive in the workplace. According to Dr. Robert Rohm, chairman and founder of Personality Insights, Inc., for I types, recognition is their secret fuel. For S types, it is appreciation, for C types it is quality answers and excellence, and for D types it is challenges and choices.[4] Knowing the secret fuel for each person on your team can give an organization an advantage, and even greater results as a team. An African proverb about teamwork states, "If you want to go fast, go alone. If you want to go far, go together."[5] In order to go together, we must understand each personality type, its motivations, and what hinders a person's productivity. Dr. John C. Maxwell reminds us that, "One is too small a number to achieve greatness. The truth is that teamwork is at the heart of great achievement."[6] These little and subtle changes have the power to increase our effectiveness as communicators and leaders.

Using the DISC Profile with Executives

This year I had the privilege to come alongside a group of busy executive women with roles in C-Suite and senior positions. Through bi-weekly networking, learning, goal setting, and support, the group focused on creating more balance between work and family life, as well as ways to be mentally and physically healthier. The DISC personality profile was one tool that I encouraged the group to examine. Although we held a group debriefing session, a few of the group members opted to debrief individually with me about their DISC experience. Many who selected to have a coaching session about their DISC results gained greater clarity on how they show up for life. They received an expanded view of themselves and how others might perceive them. The report gave them a great deal of information, but a conversation with a trained DISC consultant allowed them to process even more information, and gain an in-depth understanding of their personality blend. In addition, we entered into candid conversations about life experiences that shaped their perspectives on supervision, supporting and holding team members accountable, as well as the appropriateness of sharing intense emotions and being vulnerable in the workplace. Of all the DISC debriefings I have conducted, there was a consensus about the value of having a thinking partner in understanding the DISC tool, and a person's unique personality type. The report and debriefing helped them clarify, solidify, validate, or reconfirm their strengths, and challenged them to reexamine their blind spots and how others perceived them. One executive stated, "Reviewing my DISC report with a trusted coach was like reading a different report because it provided me with incredible insights for accepting how strong I show up and it fueled my desire to want to know myself better. It also shifted my thinking to want to further learn about my team's personality types and how they perceive me. I want to be more intentional about how I show up at work and how I interact with and support my team."

What a gift it is to be able to hold up the mirror of our behavior and truly see who we are and see how other people see us. This awareness has the potential to change our interactions with others, as we consider their "language of behavior" in efforts to increase communication. The DISC Model of Human Behavior is more than just reading people...It is about truly seeing others—their personality, temperament, tendencies, motivations, and feelings. Most importantly, it is about speaking a person's language, and bringing out the best in yourself and in others.

The DISC Model of Human Behavior helps people accept what each personality type brings to the table, allowing for greater connections and understanding. Where would the world be if we were all the same? As we find value in each personality blend that exists in the world, we gain immense insights into human behavior, people's motivations, and how we can inspire greater productivity and performance in others and ourselves. Perspective taking is key if we desire to communicate more effectively and live a life of success and significance.

Using DISC with Organizations

In a DISC workshop that I provided for a large, multi-service, nonprofit organization, we unpacked the tendencies of each personality type. Due to the size of this organization, which had layers of teams, it was helpful to share this information on personality types and how we engage people that are different from ourselves. As we went through the exercises, the participants laughed and recalled family members, colleagues, and supervisors with these traits and behaviors. What was most intriguing was what the DISC mirror revealed. "Yeah, this describes me exactly." "It was like someone got inside my head." "It seems like you know where I am coming from and where I work and live."

During another event that I facilitated for ministry leaders at a church retreat, similar comments were stated. "I learned about the different personality types that we confront every day as leaders. It was so helpful to learn about each of them. I now know that we need to learn from one another and treat each other with respect. It is okay to see things differently. I don't have to be like anyone else. I can just be me." Another participant added, "The conference helped me do a self-evaluation of 'Who am I?'. It helped me to see that we can lead people through understanding their personality types. I need to develop my D side." One participant shared, "This is so helpful for me in my marriage, in understanding my spouse more. These are wonderful takeaways that carry the messages that it is okay to be who you were created to be and not aspire to be anyone else." The DISC personality profile is an instrument that can make these types of organic conversations possible, and that can ultimately improve staff morale, employee engagement, team connectivity, productivity, and performance. Personal growth is a prerequisite for professional growth.

Finally, I want to urge you not to see the DISC personality profile as another assessment you file away, but as an empowerment mirror that reflects your heart to others, and validates who you truly are. Knowing what the DISC Model of Human Behavior reveals about the diversity of both personality and thinking modalities can set us up to be more intentional about perspective taking, and our own communication styles. It can help us to value the viewpoints of others and not dismiss them just because they do not match our own. The DISC Model of Human Behavior can serve us well as leaders and as citizens of the world. We can agree that all personality types are valuable, and that each type brings us information leading to an unlimited perspective of the complexity of human behavior; it provides the bandwidth and tools to allow others to shine the way they were designed to shine. This is the advantage of the DISC Model of Human Behavior, along with the study of your unique personality style with a trained coach.

ABOUT ANA BERDECÍA

Ana I. Berdecía, M.Ed., Founder and CEO of Potential Pathways, LLC., has been a growth expert for thirty years. She has helped hundreds of people and organizations improve their culture, communications, productivity, performance, and employee engagement. Her company offers life and leadership coaching, team building seminars, retreat facilitation, Lunch-N-Learns, masterminds, and leadership assessments. Berdecía uses her gifts to inspire people to find their strengths, positioning them toward excellence through the art of facilitated conversations. She believes that passion and potential are the gateways to taking leaders and their companies to new heights and innovative solutions.

Throughout her career, Berdecía has worked in social services, crisis management, nonprofit support, higher education, and public policy. She earned both a master's in education and a bachelor of art in sociology with a minor in women studies from The College of New Jersey. She holds a standard teaching certificate and a certificate in nonprofit management. As a master teacher/trainer, she has taught courses and seminars in education, leadership, mentoring/coaching, cultural competency, communication, and leading effective teams. In addition, Berdecía is an independent certified coach, speaker, and trainer with the John Maxwell International Team and a Certified Human Behavior Consultant.

Website: https://www.potentialpathways.com

LinkedIn: www.linkedin.com/in/coach-ana-growthexpert

Chapter Thirteen

Understanding Tomorrow's Leaders, Today

Steve Goble

Everything rises and falls with leadership. - John C. Maxwell

If you look around our world, you'll see the above quote from my friend and mentor, John Maxwell, is true. From politics and business to education and our lives, a large percentage of our success or failure is derived from our ability as leaders.

I'm not a millennial, but I'm tired of all the millennial bashing within the media and business community. It's the lazy way of telling the world you have no idea how to adapt and address the challenges and opportunities the next generation brings.

When you take advantage of the information available through a DISC behavioral analysis, you lose any excuse that has allowed you to be lazy; you also enhance the opportunity to serve others, and you begin to build your organization into something stronger and more effective—an organization that is thriving, and not just surviving. With this information for greater understanding readily available, why are we lacking so many qualified leaders throughout our governments, our educational system, and our businesses?

Part of it is a lack of awareness about the information available, part of it is the lack of intentionality in our daily choices, and part of it is the discomfort leadership brings into our lives because the responsibilities associated with leadership disrupt our sense of normalcy.

If you don't think you're a leader because you don't have a title, you don't have a nice corner office, or you're not plastered all over social media, I challenge you to look in the mirror. *At the bare minimum, you're a leader of yourself.* Former President

Theodore "Teddy" Roosevelt famously said, "If you could kick the person in the pants responsible for most of your trouble, you wouldn't sit for a month."

As current leaders who want to grow, who want to get better, and who wish to gain a better understanding of the future generations, the first place we have to look is in the mirror. We must take the initiative to understand ourselves well.

Leadership is scarce because few people are willing to go through the discomfort required to lead. - Seth Godin

As a High D behavioral style, I can't help you much with your personal intentions or the discomfort you may feel solely through reading this book. However, I can share a few simple concepts that, combined with a proper assessment of yourself and your team, will help you along the leadership journey as you build and strengthen relationships in both your personal, and professional life.

I call these the "***Five L's of Leadership***".

1. Listen

God gave us two ears and one mouth, yet we use our mouths more frequently than our ears; and more often than not, to our own detriment. What happens to us when we focus on listening? How does this backward strategy help us to learn more about others so we can begin to lay the foundation for a healthy, mutually beneficial relationship?

The next time you go into a meeting or networking event, display honest humility and focus on listening to others; don't focus as much on yourself. Don't be thinking about your response while the other person is still talking. If you're actively listening, your response will come more easily because you're focusing not only on the words that are being said, but also on the tone and body language of the speaker, as well as the context within which the words are being said. The self-discipline required to listen will not only set you apart from others, but it will also help you learn more about the behavioral style of the person you're listening to, and will give you extra information you can use to help add value to your relationship with that person.

What are tomorrow's leaders trying to tell us right now that we might not be paying enough attention to because we're not listening? Are they suggesting improvements that leaders of today aren't picking up on, or are we just failing to act on their suggestions? We must be willing to act on what we're hearing; however, we can only do that if we don't dismiss others so quickly, and actually listen to them.

You'll be surprised how many people will feel appreciated that you listened to them, and what that newfound insight can lead to as it relates to personal and professional success for everyone involved.

2. Learn

Whether you have co-workers, or you supervise any number of employees, it's essential to learn about them, professionally and personally. I don't think you need to go all *Jason Bourne* on them, but if you truly listen to them, you'll be able to learn so much more about them, and be able to apply this understanding in new ways that help unlock their potential. When you invest the time to learn about the people around you through active listening, the first thing you'll come to understand is that everyone is not the same!

I'm the proud dad of daughter, Dani, and son, Kai. Even though they're both my biological children, and are a little less than three-and-a-half years apart in age, they are different children through and through. It doesn't mean I love one more than the other, but it does mean I have to know how to parent each of them differently based on several factors, most notably their behavioral tendencies. I know that to provide the most for my kids, I need to encourage each of them, and support them in their areas of strengths, while simultaneously challenging them to be aware of others around them as they're completing their chores and studies, or embarking on new adventures.

By no means do I have this whole parenting thing figured out, but I do know that in terms of my professional life, many people who hire me are frustrated by the "babysitting" they feel they have to do with their teams on a daily basis. However, the change to this "babysitting" feeling starts with today's leaders and their behaviors.

When you tailor your leadership style to the strengths of your team—through a better understanding of their individual styles—your leadership ability will increase. You'll have to do less babysitting, and the results your team achieves will increase in a positive way.

3. Love

Love is an action verb; you need to show love to your team, even if they sometimes don't deserve it. Yes, I know our emotions make it hard to do this, especially after a mistake or during a financial crisis, but it's important.

When I first moved to Lancaster, Pennsylvania after college, I worked as a store manager in a new business within a tourist village. The space had previously been used to sell handcrafted furniture—we're talking about unique bedroom suites, desks, and high-end pieces that cost in the thousands of dollars. The furniture was meticulously built, stained, and loved.

Only, I didn't know any better about the quality, care, and skill that had been used to create that furniture. A price list hadn't been provided to me...I was just given instructions that one of my tasks was to get rid of the old inventory that the current owner had obtained as part of the buy-out of the retiring craftsman's space.

One of the first weekends our new store was open, I sold an exquisitely crafted, six-drawer oak desk for $700 or so—and I was super excited! That is, until I told the owner of the store. He wasn't nearly as excited, as that particular desk should have sold for closer to $2500! As a newly-minted store manager, I had just made a substantial financial mistake, and my boss could have yelled at me, or even fired me. Rather than do either of those things, he showed me a little love and explained in depth what I had done wrong, and helped me understand how valuable the furniture was. He also got me a price list for the remaining inventory!

Looking back, even though I felt anxious for a short period after, this was a great learning experience for me. I continued to work for that boss for four years, helping to build a brand-new store from the ground up, while sharing love to clients and team members alike. I was able to do this because I knew I had screwed up, but I also knew that when I had mishaps in the future, I would still be offered a little bit of love.

When your team causes a mistake, especially a large financial one, they'll be very appreciative that you took time to show them love when they probably weren't feeling so hot about themselves. That love will be reciprocated many times over when the mistake is long forgotten, or the financial challenge from that mistake has been overcome.

4. Lead

It's not enough to just talk about leadership: it must be an action lived out daily. How, you ask? Get the right set of decision makers in the room, explain the situation you're in, discuss potential solutions, challenges, and outcomes, and then decide. Sounds simple, right? Please don't make the mistake of thinking that simple is synonymous with easy!

Understanding who the right decision-makers are, the role they want to play based on their behavioral style and positional title, and the people they can best influence will put you in a better position to make the correct decision as the leader.

When you make any decision as a leader, you have to be sure that everyone working with you, or those affected by the decision, have the same expectations as you in relation to the execution of the decision, and putting it into action. This requires you as the leader to be prepared to manage others' ROE ("Return on Expectations") so you're not caught off guard based on others' behavior as it relates to the results. As a leader, you must *own* your decision (whether you're right or wrong) based on the results that decision produces.

Ultimately, in a healthy and productive organization, your leadership will be judged based on the results you bring to the table, and so the ability to understand those helping you to make important decisions are vital to your success.

Remember...You're not perfect, and nobody expects you to get it right 100 percent of the time. However, if you're consistent with the first three L's as part of your leadership style, and you've consistently shown love to those you collaborate with, members of your team and your boss should be able to offer a little grace when it's warranted.

5. Let Go

Many so-called "leaders" cling to a title or the idea that being a leader means power alone. Instead of growing their team, insecure leaders hover over and smother team members, taking away the desire individuals have to create. This clingy type of leadership couldn't be further from the true idea of leadership; it simultaneously ends up chasing away your best people, and diminishing your true potential as a leader, and an organization.

What does your team look like? Do you have the right people in the right roles that complement each other due to their behavioral style and skill sets? Or do you have too many people on your team who want to be in charge, and not enough who actually get the job done?

If you're a fan of sports, you know that on the best teams, players know their role and are expected to play that role. Do they sometimes need to fill in and help out a teammate to get the job done? Absolutely! But once the help is given, they go back to the original role for which they were put on the team. This need to include diverse talent on your team means you need to personally let go of tasks or obligations that might be better suited for others. Just because you can, doesn't mean you should!

Will letting go of some things lead to mistakes? Potentially.

Will letting go of some things help people discover more of themselves, giving them more experience and confidence in the process? Absolutely.

When Sir Richard Branson shared his belief that businesses should "train people well enough so they can leave, treat them well enough so they don't want to," he was onto something. The more likely outcome is that the long-term rewards and loyalty are worth the risks of delegating some responsibilities to your team members.

In summary, while the five points I've outlined are simple in concept, it doesn't mean they're always easy to accomplish, and they are almost impossible to do without a deeper understanding of your team, and their behavioral tendencies. If you do these five things consistently and with intentionality, combining them with a guiding voice of understanding and development, over time, you'll grow into a well-respected leader.

As a well-respected leader, your primary responsibility is to build up and develop others so that they are able to assume the leadership responsibilities and opportunities that are coming—responsibilities and opportunities that in reality, are already there.

To truly evaluate and increase your ability to *"Understand Tomorrow's Leader's, Today,"* you have to balance your need for ROI (return on investment) with the corresponding COI (cost of inaction). Ignoring a problem won't make it go away. Understanding the behavioral nature of your team is the place to start, and I'd love to assist you in solving problems, and building strong people.

ABOUT STEVE GOBLE

Steve is the Owner/Chief People Builder at the Goble Group. As a speaker, teacher, and certified coach, Steve helps individuals work through the realization that our lives and relationships won't always be easy, but they're always an adventure. Steve understands that the more high tech we become, the more high touch we will need to be, and he uses a personal touch to help his clients reach their goals.

Steve is a firm believer that an organization is only as strong as its people—internal team members and external customers—and their ability to interact with one another to accomplish the tasks at hand and get the positive results needed to succeed. As the people grow, so grows the organization, and Steve helps the people to grow.

Steve is Founding Partner of the John Maxwell Team, a Certified Human Behavior Consultant, and was a 2017 "Forty Under 40" recipient from the *Central Penn Business Journal*. Steve currently resides in Lancaster County, Pennsylvania, with his family, where he enjoys petting other people's dogs and a good pint of IPA. No, he and his family are not Amish.

Connect with Steve:

LinkedIn: https://www.linkedin.com/in/gobles/

Email: steve@thegoblegroup.com

Phone: 717.682.3198

Chapter Fourteen

Moving from Good to Better to Best

Jelena Simpson

"Coming together is a beginning. Keeping together is progress. Working together is success." - Henry Ford

A couple of years ago, we took a family vacation to Italy. While there, I noticed that in restaurants, the waitstaff do not bring water to the table when you sit down like they do in the United States. Instead, they asked if you would like natural (not sparkling) or gassata (carbonated fizzy) water, and then brought you a bottle based on your answer. This got me thinking: Is there a right answer to that question? Why do some choose one over the other? There is no "right" answer to the question, just our preference.

While working alongside my clients throughout the years, whether it has been with professionals in healthcare, legal areas, sales, executives, or businesses and individuals, all have different stories, perspectives, and personalities on their teams. So how do we best adapt in the business world and in our personal lives to interpret all the different perspectives and communication styles which have such great power—for better or worse—to impact our team or business? I have repeatedly seen firsthand how DISC leads to a better understanding of others, so that effective communication can take place and generate cooperation and top performance, leading to numerous benefits in professional and personal life. Knowing that communication is crucial, when I take on a new client, I first use the DISC model to discover where a client's behavior style lies and how best to communicate. Some people are take-charge problem solvers, while others might be more focused on fun, stability, or hard facts and making logical decisions. DISC allows us to create a connection with a common language, and then approach the coaching process based on a mutual understanding of how the client and I can best work together toward success. DISC is not just for business relationships—it is also useful personally. We interact with people every day on a personal level, be it our children, spouse, neighbors, or just some random person we meet while ordering coffee. Have you ever had a conversation with someone and thought afterward, "Well, that didn't go as planned"? Do you look back on that conversation and think you could have handled it differently, or that the other person could have handled it differently? We all have patterns and habits embedded in our daily lives based on how we think and feel. While we have our primary comfort zone, we do not always stay in that natural zone. External factors, such as stress or a crisis, can and often times does, affect our method of communication. By learning and utilizing DISC tools, we can train ourselves, teams, and organizations to be stronger, less reactionary, and to experience less tension when times get stressful and we fall out of our primary comfort zone.

I have found that the top training and resource leading to better communication and cohesion for me, as well as for teams, organizations, and individuals is the DISC Behavioral Model. It simplifies the understanding of how every one of us is "wired"— how we respond to our environment and people around us. There are four styles in the DISC Model. They are: D, I, S and C. Each style has identifying features such as individual strengths, group strengths, danger zones, and fears. It also goes much deeper. We all have a blend of the styles, and each blend affects our behavior in certain situations. Stress might bring out someone's D style when they usually are an S style. Now you might be wondering what these letters mean...Briefly, without going into too much detail, the D style is the Dominant style; people in this style are outgoing and task oriented. The I style is the Inspiring style; people in this style are outgoing and people-oriented. The S style is the Supportive style; people in this style are reserved and people-oriented. The C style is the Cautious style; people in this style are reserved and task-oriented. As you can probably see, there are overlapping traits in each of the four quadrants. So, this means that each of us has a unique way of interacting with our environment based upon where our personality lies within the quadrants.

Now you are saying, "Wow! That's so simple!" But in reality, here we can start to dig a little deeper. In my years as a trainer and professional business coach, I have used the DISC Behavioral Model as a "jumping off" point to launch my clients on the road from "good" to "better" to "best." Everyone likes to be in their comfort zone—or in the words of the DISC model—they like to stay in their primary style. We are comfortable there, and it's where we function the best in everyday life; that is our "good" area. But with a little more training and understanding, we can also focus on our secondary and tertiary styles, which are the styles that usually come to the forefront when stress shows up in our lives. With further understanding of our secondary and tertiary styles, we move to "better." When we account for all of our blended styles and use them to avoid misalignments, as well as to enhance our communication and interaction with those around us, we have moved from "better" to "best."

Enhancing communication and interaction with those around us is an ongoing process. Frequently, I am asked to perform DISC assessments for teams. After completing the assessment, I walk them through their results, explaining what it all means. But then the training often stops because people have their pieces of paper in hand, but then do nothing with the information. Even though they now have the tools, they usually stop short, and do not fully utilize them. There are those who pursue deeper understanding, training, and practical application...They are moving toward "best" with their success. I once had a psychotherapist client who ordered DISC assessments for their team. Being psychotherapists, they understood a great deal about personalities, effective communication, and conflict resolution, but even they were shocked with how the DISC Behavioral Model provided them with a new framework to view their communication and leadership styles. We met weekly for six months, during which we explored and dug deeper into their

127

individual assessments, and how they pertained to the team dynamics. We explored how leadership styles could contribute to, or even hinder the team; we discussed their styles and strengths, but we also discussed their blind spots. Blind spots are the areas of our personality which we may or may not be aware of. The understanding of blind spots is a key component that leads to helping teams navigate interpersonal dynamics with an increased level of self-awareness. We also focused on each person's individual DISC style so that it became much easier to depersonalize any challenges due to style differences. Understanding and recognizing these differences provides the opportunity for open discussion and better collaboration, capitalizing on the strengths of each team member. Through continuous training, we worked on the practical application, from the details obtained in their DISC profiles through interactive exercises that focused on managing expectations to limit backsliding into old comfort zones.

The beauty of the DISC Behavioral Model is that it appears so simple, yet is so very complex if you take the time to understand it fully. I think that is what attracts so many people to it. The model, if you dig deep enough and take the time to really understand the information contained in each personal report, can really be a fantastic tool to help build team synergy and cohesiveness.

While I have used the DISC Behavior Model many times in the professional world, I also have had the opportunity to use it in my personal life. My DISC style blend is I/DS, which means my behavior type is outgoing and people-oriented. I like to jump right into a problem and solve it as fast as possible, while providing encouragement and building team harmony. But processes can be inconsequential to me. In contrast, my son likes to be prepared with facts and details. His DISC style blend is C/SD: the specifics of a task are essential to him. He likes to have time to think about a problem, be a team player, and move at a predictable, slower pace. While we have overlapping traits, at a quick glance, he looks to be the exact opposite of me!

Every morning, when getting ready for school, my son likes to prepare by asking what the current temperature is, as well as what the high and low is going to be for the day so that he can dress appropriately. Without much thought, when he was younger, I would rush into his room and say, "Hurry up, it's time to go!" I would quickly offer solutions, like finding his socks and shoes, and rush him out of the house. We were hurried, creating unnecessary stress, and felt rushed getting ready for the day. So, as he got older, I communicated more effectively with him by giving him a five-minute warning, believing that would give him plenty of time and then he would be ready to go. Well, we were still moving at my pace and not his, which frustrated both of us. He complained that he felt rushed, like he was forgetting something, or doing a "half-job," and that he was not doing things "correctly." As I became more aware of communication styles and studying behavioral types, I would catch myself saying things that were not effective in dealing with him and his methodical pace. I really struggled with being patient with him. After comparing both of our DISC assessments, I found that now we had a starting point in which to address areas that were making our communication less effective. I implemented some new ideas, keeping in mind his behavioral type, to improve our daily process in a "better" way. First, I asked questions. For example, "How long do you think you need to wake up, take a shower, eat breakfast, and be ready to go?" And then I gave him the opportunity to respond after he had some time to think about it. Keeping his answers in mind, I changed my behavior in the mornings by walking into his room, and while checking the weather on my phone, I would state, "It is 6:33 a.m., currently fifty-two degrees outside, and the high is going to be seventy-three degrees. We need to be ready and out the door in one hour." I left the room feeling pretty proud of myself. I intentionally chose another and better way based on his style and increased our communication. He got what he needed from our conversation, and I was, hopefully, going to get what I needed as well, which was to have a more peaceful morning routine together.

Now, because he is a High C style, not thirty seconds passed before he poked his head out of the door and said, "Mom, we actually have to leave at 7:30 a.m."

I thought, "Seriously! You are going to correct me over a three-minute difference?" In the past, a similar situation like this might have me responding defensively, ending with me snapping at him, and I may have even shut him down and told him not to correct me. However, according to his DISC behavioral style, his High C needs precision and accuracy, while my High I does not. Remembering this, I realized my statement about the departure time was not "correct" in his eyes, but what I said was not wrong in my eyes either...We just have different styles when it comes to communication. I had been focusing on my way of communicating, not his way. I said, "You're right," and adjusted my morning communications with him to include the exact time we need to leave, as opposed to how much time he has to get ready, and it seems to be working well. We are rarely rushed in the mornings anymore. Maintaining good communication is an ongoing exercise. My son and I have continuing conversations in an effort to manage expectations and the gaps in communication that are highlighted by our behavioral styles.

There is no perfect solution when it comes to communication. It is inevitable that we all have similarities, differences, and tensions directly tied to our unique personality types and how we communicate, whether we are at our best or not. With the DISC Behavioral Model, training, and practice, I love to help foster better communication. I have seen firsthand how DISC impacts and leads us to a better understanding of others so that effective communication can take place, leading to "best" practices in professional and personal life. I welcome the opportunity to share this fantastic resource, support you in bridging the gap, and increase your success while you transition smoothly from good to better to best.

ABOUT JELENA SIMPSON

Professionally trained, licensed, and certified, Jelena's passion is to empower, encourage, and equip others for transformational development—both in business and life! Challenging growth processes stretch our comfort zones, but Jelena is with you every step of the way as you create clarity, develop goals, and implement best practices to transition from good to better to best.

Jelena's international services to enhance productivity and transformation include: team development, business and leadership coaching, corporate training, mentoring, and speaking. Jelena has been an active member of executive and management teams, giving her considerable insight into understanding organizational needs. Jelena has worked in both the private and public sectors with the best and brightest people as a confidante and trusted advisor since 1996.

She is twenty-three years happily married, with one son and a dog. Jelena was raised on a working ranch in West Texas, where values for family, integrity, and hard work were learned! Travel, reading, and service work are her pastimes.

Jelena's goal is to find something to laugh about daily...and she has fulfillment knowing she has a place and plan to help others. She founded Jelena Simpson Consulting to help you, too, and invites you to connect today: info@jelenasimpson.com or www.jelenasimpson.com.

Chapter Fifteen

Use DISC to Personalize Instruction to Achieve Massive Student Academic Performance Growth

Carla Gray, Ph.D.

As a preteen during the long, hot, and humid Mississippi summers of the late 1970s, I would find myself playing "superheroes" with my older brother and neighborhood friends to pass the time. They would enact Spiderman, Superman, The Incredible Hulk, and the villains. I portrayed Wonder Woman. Wearing my blue jean short pants, a red tank top, and white knee-high tube socks, I dressed the part. I accessorized my makeshift costume with my spray-painted gold-colored belt that gave me tremendous strength, my gold stretch wrist bands that I used to deflect pretend bullets, and a gold headband that was a defensive weapon. To gain an advantage over suspects who attempted to disguise the truth from me, I accessorized myself with my special weapon, the Lasso of Truth, which was actually just an old jump rope that I had spray-painted gold. Even though my fashion design skills were limited, I was determined to look the part.

While playing "superheroes," I would spin around in a circle to fully transform and to garner my superpowers. Twirling my lasso, I would chase the villains who had allegedly committed crimes. Once I had captured them with my lasso, I would interrogate them with a series of questions that helped me understand the truth about their criminal intentions. During my preteen years, I was intrigued with transforming myself into my favorite superhero. As an adult, I find myself even more fascinated with not only discovering the truth within others, but revealing the truth inside myself in order to make a positive impact on the world around me.

In recent years, to my amazement, Wonder Woman has become a part of my adult life through a most unusual source. While awaiting the start of an evening church service, I struck up a conversation with a prominent, retired school superintendent who was sitting in the church pew in front of me. Even though we had attended the same church for several years, we had not formally met. After the retired school superintendent learned that I was CEO of my own educational consulting firm, she shared with me her testimony regarding her former school district's success during her tenure in the early 1990s. She further expressed a major concern as it related to the drastic academic decline that the school district had taken since her retirement. She sparked my interest when she exclaimed that the significant performance growth that her school district experienced during her tenure was a direct result of applying William Marston's Model of Human Behavior, better known as DISC, to personalize their approach to leadership and teaching instruction in the classroom. I was so inspired and motivated by her testimony, I started researching DISC the very next day. The more that I learned about the effectiveness and benefits of DISC, the more elated I became. Never in a million years could I have imagined what I would discover as I sifted through the research. I discovered that William Marston was not only the creator of DISC, but he was also the creator of my favorite childhood superhero, Wonder Woman.

With research in hand and a welcomed reunion between me and my childhood memories of pretending to be Wonder Woman, I knew adding DISC to my company's offerings was the superpower that we needed to truly impact schools. For nearly twenty years, our company, Educational Treasures, LLC, had been committed to adding value to schools in the areas of curriculum development, school administrators' and teachers' professional development, and teacher coaching. Adding DISC to our process could only elevate our offerings and profoundly impact administrators, teachers, and students. Becoming certified in DISC would be my next step.

Locating the appropriate DISC Certification Program was essential. With hundreds of companies offering DISC certification training, it was important to collaborate with a company that aligned with our company's values and beliefs. Making the telephone call to Chris Rollins, one of the owners of Rollins Performance Group, was one of the most life-changing calls that I have ever made. He assured me that their DISC certification process would be transformational and exceed my expectations.

The DISC certification process was both fascinating and profound. While taking a DISC Assessment during the certification training, I had a major flashback. *Deja Vu! Is this the magic lasso that I used to get the truth from the assailants that I captured when I pretended to be Wonder Woman during my preteen years?* In retrospect, I never used the Lasso of Truth on myself to examine my own truths. Nevertheless, the DISC assessment process was a simulation of the Lasso of Truth experience. For each of the twenty-four questions on the self-assessment, I selected one line of words that LEAST described me and one line of words that MOST described me. As a result of answering the questions on the DISC assessment, I received a DISC Profile Report that revealed truths about my behaviors. The profile revealed truly accurate descriptions of my strengths, predictable behaviors, and communication style.

My DISC Profile Report revealed that I have major strengths that are empowering and "blind spots" that need slight adjustments. To describe my personality, my profile stated that I am Supportive, Cautious, and Inspiring, also known as the SC/I style blend. As an SC/I style blend, I am highly helpful when working with teams, and I am very attentive to details. Another strength is that I can be extremely influential when working with people. However, it was shocking to learn that when I am under pressure or in stressful environments, I naturally become less dominant, which was depicted as one of my "blind spots." Learning about the strengths and "blind spots" of my personality style blend motivated me to become more productive by adjusting my behavior in the areas of communication, relationship building, team building, and conflict management.

After becoming certified in DISC, I challenged myself to apply the concepts in my everyday life on a personal level. It was my mission to learn everything possible about DISC before presenting it to consultants and instructional coaches who worked with my company. I wanted to have my own testimony regarding its effectiveness, as well as a personal proof of concept.

Like most families, my husband, my daughter, and I have experienced challenges in the area of communication due to differences in our personalities. My teenage daughter and I have similar communication style blends with varying degrees on each trait, while my husband has a completely opposite style blend. These differences used to bring about stress from time to time.

After learning the process from the DISC certification training for adjusting my style of communicating to the desired communication styles of other people, I transferred the knowledge to my daughter and husband. I taught my daughter to provide me with a detailed action plan that included a description of how she is going to complete her homework assignments or chores, including time frames, when communicating with me. Furthermore, I underscored the importance of her using the same process when planning outings with her friends and communicating her itinerary with me. Understanding *how* something is going to be completed is one of my greatest needs. This process satisfies my High S type. On the other hand, to suffice her High C type, my daughter needed me to provide logical supporting evidence answering the question, "Why?" She and I shared our desired language with my husband, her dad, who is hard wired as a High D type. My daughter and I learned to communicate with her dad in terms of what we planned to do using facts with minimal explanation rather than *how* or *why* we were going to carry out a plan. Learning each other's desired language changed our family communication patterns tremendously. We now experience more peace and harmony in our family and home. This is such a powerful process for improving the communication in any family structure, from both the husband-to-wife relationship and the parent-to-child relationship perspectives.

After consistently using DISC with my family, I gained massive personal growth development in the areas of self-awareness, communication, relationship building, leadership influence, team building skills, and conflict management. I was truly prepared to use it with my company's educational consultants and coaches. My goal was to train my colleagues, and then to create a system using DISC to add more value to schools.

Over the years, my company has successfully assisted hundreds of schools in customizing their curricula for the purpose of improving student academic performance growth. To support the implementation of the customized curricula, we have provided onsite professional training and instructional teacher coaching. Typically, our focus has been to support schools in delivering effective and quality instruction using profound strategies and models of teaching in classrooms. Adding DISC to our service offerings would empower us to not only assist teachers in teaching curricula, but also assist them in personalizing instruction according to the way their students process information and make decisions.

When designing our system to add value to schools using DISC, I kept one major factor in the forefront. On average, there is only a 40 percent chance that a person's personality and communication style naturally fit or match that of another person.[1] This one factor can present major challenges for both teachers and students. Even when teachers have high-quality instructional delivery, differences between the teachers' communication styles and that of their students can impede the learning process. As a result of this difference, a large percentage of students face extreme frustration and poor academic performance. Subsequently, students are often forced to obtain support through after-school tutoring, or hopelessly give up. As a by-product of this crisis, a possible increase in disciplinary problems, chronic school absenteeism, school suspensions, school expulsions, and school dropout rates is likely to occur across the board.

In efforts to provide a solution to this widespread problem, our company developed a three-tier system that we titled, "Success Formula: Personalizing Instruction for Massive Performance Growth." Our Success Formula is designed to empower schools to ensure student mastery of 21st Century Learning, Literacy, and Life Skills, as well as College and Career Readiness Standards.[2] It focuses on three major components: (1) understanding ourselves, (2) understanding others, and (3) adjusting ourselves to others. This focus is the foundation for our three-tier process that addresses: effective school leadership, personalized teacher instruction, and massive student academic performance growth.

For school success to occur, leadership must be effective. In his book, *The 21 Irrefutable Laws of Leadership*, John Maxwell (2007) highlights the importance of the Law of Connection. The Law of Connection states, "Leaders touch a heart before they ask for a hand."[3] Tier One of our Success Formula is designed to use DISC Leadership Profile data collected from school leaders to positively impact school performance. School leaders acquire the ability to predict the actions and reactions of other people. They learn to understand the style blends of their support staff, teachers, students, and community members. Leaders both influence and impact others through effective relationships, team building, and conflict management.

Relationship building is essential to educating students. Tier Two of our Success Formula is designed to empower teachers in building strong relationships with students, as well as with their own family members, friends, and colleagues. Using DISC Adult Profile and Student Profile data, teachers obtain an understanding of themselves and their students. Teachers and students then learn to accept and appreciate each other's talents and gifts.

Tier Three of our Success Formula personalizes lesson plans and instructional delivery in the classroom through coaching. A Student DISC Profile that provides descriptions of each student's style blend is provided to teachers, students, and parents. Teachers gain knowledge about how each student processes

138

information and makes decisions. For example, people with High D tendencies learn best by discovering things for themselves, whereas people with High S tendencies learn best following a step-by-step process. Once teachers, students, and parents understand the way every person makes decisions and processes information, instruction can then be tailored to each individual student.[4]

Many students are not being reached in classrooms because their personality and communication styles do not naturally match their teachers' communication styles. DISC gives both teachers and students the tools and language they need to adjust to each other's styles. When teachers adjust instruction to meet each student's desired communication style and mode of learning using DISC profile data, they become superheroes. Ultimately, students achieve massive performance growth.

ABOUT CARLA GRAY, Ph.D.

Dr. Carla Gray is Founder and CEO of Educational Treasures, LLC. Having been in business since 1999, she has provided countless individuals, business professionals, and school district staff members with resources, coaching, and professional training that has led to high performance and high achievement.

Dr. Gray is an entrepreneur who is a certified coach and trainer for DISC: The Model of Human Behavior. She designed the system, *Success Formula: Personalizing Instruction for Massive Performance*, to empower school districts to achieve massive student academic growth. Using DISC, Dr. Gray designs customized trainings and programs that revolutionize educational institutions, small businesses, entrepreneurs, community organizations, and organizational teams.

Dr. Gray holds specialized certifications and has worked in a number of educational capacities. She is certified in Leadership, Curriculum and Instruction, Elementary Education, and K-12 Reading Instruction. She has worked as a State Department of Education curriculum and instruction coordinator, Central Office curriculum coordinator, principal, and teacher.

Dr. Gray's greatest passion is empowering people by giving them the KEY to unlock their GREATNESS!

Chapter Sixteen

How DISC Could Have Helped the Department of... EVERYTHING

Jim Costey

"The art of communication is the language of leadership" - *James Humes*

Learning and understanding the different languages associated with human behavior was one of the most impactful leadership lessons I have ever experienced. Building upon psychologist William Marston's DISC theory as published in *The Emotions of Normal People*[1], Robert Rohm, Ph.D. expanded upon the Model of Human Behavior by demonstrating that each personality style communicates with its own unique language. The ability to understand and adapt to each communication style is a powerful tool for becoming a highly successful leader and team member.

Throughout nearly thirty years of working in a myriad of leadership roles, I believe I developed into a highly effective leader. I can point to ribbons on a rack, awards received, and promotions as bona fides of my belief, but those items are tokens that represent the results of the great work achieved by the teams of which I was a part. My development was the result of others investing in me in such a way that they awakened my awareness of who I was, and what I could become. Before it was understood, they helped me identify "my why" and taught me that growth is continuous and comes through taking risks, reflecting on the results, and implementing changes in my life from those lessons learned.

Those lessons learned included the importance of humility, recognizing how critical the diversity of experience and thought are, time management, effective communication, identifying the needs of others and placing those needs above my own, and so many others. Many of those lessons learned came through deliberate learning: the implementation of Steven Covey's *Seven Habits of Highly Effective People*, as well as applying elements from multiple leadership biographies and leadership books from authors like James Hunter, John C. Maxwell, and Simon Sinek. All inspired me to discover my gaps, and to seek continuous improvement; however, none of them had the impact on me that learning about DISC did. The DISC certification process was the only training that made me think, "Boy, I wish I had known this years ago."

During DISC certification, I had epiphany after epiphany; if they were fireworks, it would have been the equivalent of a Fourth of July celebration. Throughout the training, I gained incredible insight into who I am, and why I am the way I am. Equally important, I gained insight into the who and why of other personality styles. I learned that my DISC personality style blend is C/S. I learned where my blind spots are, how to work through them, and how to best engage with other personality styles to better enable their success. As I learned, I realized that had I understood DISC and applied it a few years earlier, I could have completely changed the failing dynamics I experienced with a past supervisor.

A few years ago, I found myself in a fantastic leadership opportunity, which was potentially the most significant leadership challenge I had ever faced. I was selected to build a new organization (with new and experienced employees) designed to carry out a new vision of customer service. I was empowered to be creative in finding solutions while also bringing customers back to operating within federal guidelines. In other words, I was living the leadership dream of building a new organization—new vision, new culture, new rules of engagement—with the ultimate goal of achieving a level of service not seen before within our supported community. For context, the organization was a Human Resources (HR) Service Support Center (SSC) that supported 3,500 employees, located at five geographically separated locations across the continental United States. The team of 70 HR professionals was also located across the United States, and I was geographically isolated from 95 percent of my customers, 80 percent of my team, and 100 percent of my senior leadership (who were located with 70 percent of my customers). Oh, and by the way, a majority of the customers were not on board with this new concept.

Despite the unique construct, I believed I was better prepared for this leadership opportunity than any other in my professional career. I chose to take a risk, and walked away from a comfortable, safe, corporate job, to temporarily separate from my family, and to step into a high paced, high demand, somewhat "dysfunctional" community. I did so with a genuine belief that we would be successful in delivering highly efficient and highly effective services to our supported community. Statistically, on paper, the team delivered. In the first six months of operating, the team exceeded expectations and reached milestone levels of effectiveness that we did not anticipate reaching for at least eighteen months.

As mentioned, my DISC personality style blend is C/S. The C personality style is one that is prone to asking lots of questions, and is highly reflective in the quest to ensure that decisions are well informed, have a high probability of success, and are easily defendable. C style personalities are also prone to provide highly detailed answers to questions, and they have a strong desire (or need) to follow rules, giving them a high sense of accountability for themselves and others. Lastly, a C personality style lives for research, and for gathering information, and cannot wait to share all of the information accumulated in as many PowerPoint slides as necessary to convey the topic. Cs also hate being wrong—which is another reason for their in-depth research. An S personality style is more prone to be people-oriented than task-oriented; they seek harmony across the organization, and are very likely to step in and offer assistance whenever someone needs it. Typically, not only does the S personality style not like change, it often resists change. And like most Cs, they avoid conflict and prefer not to be the center of attention. Words that best describe a C/S personality are: deliberate, humble, inclusive, loyal, thorough, kind, independent, and obstinate.[2]

My operational supervisor (chief of operations) at the time, who I believed to be a C/D personality blend (based on personal observation), and I saw eye to eye when she was fulfilling her role as the compliance officer, responsible for enforcing compliance within federal and legal guidelines. When you consider that we are both C blended personality styles, it makes sense that when it came to compliance and accountability, we would be in agreement and would wonder why everyone did not want to operate within required standards. However, when her role changed from compliance to operations, her secondary D personality style took over, and we quickly shifted from a highly effective team to one that was frequently at odds with each other.

Unlike the C personality style, D personality styles are much more focused on completing tasks, and making quick decisions; they have a higher acceptance of risk. The D personality style only wants key relevant facts, not long, in-depth discussions based on deep elements of logic, research, pros, and/or cons. They are about action: making things happen, and getting results. Like the C style, they are more task- than people-oriented.

When the operations chief transitioned roles from compliance to operations, I was excited as I believed we would work very effectively together. I was wrong. When the transition occurred, her personality style transitioned from being compliance-focused to being task-focused and much less risk averse. Every meeting, every phone call, every e-mail was about the completion of tasks, regardless of the costs, and regardless of the individual interpretation of higher-level guidance. I was surprised by the new aggressive leadership style and what appeared to be a complete shift away from compliance standards. The changes in her behavior and my lack of ability to understand them resulted in increasing tensions and, ultimately, a dysfunctional relationship.

Remember...at the time of this story taking place, I did not know of DISC, or the four primary personality styles within DISC; nor did I understand the different motivators, environmental needs, or how to best communicate with each style. During my DISC certification training, it became incredibly clear how an understanding of the primary DISC personality styles and their blends would have led me to a very different communication strategy which I believe would have resulted in a very different end state. With an understanding of the DISC personality styles and their blends, I would have recognized the transition from C-styled behavior to D-styled behavior that coincided with the transition in roles. Recognizing the change would have led to a different style of engagement due to a shift in needs from being the compliance officer to being the chief of operations.

As a compliance officer, a C/D personality style blend is right at home. The C personality style thrives in an environment with clearly defined tasks, time and resources to accomplish the task, and the opportunity to work with a team, all the while performing low-risk tasks. As the compliance officer, our meetings were highly supportive and engaging because we were speaking the same language: we were both speaking the language of the C personality style. When she transitioned to the operations chief role—a highly visible, high-pressure role, where conflict with customers was a regular daily activity—she understandably began to function more like a D personality style leader. In an attempt to reduce conflict, she uncharacteristically started making quick decisions, began redefining levels of compliance to create shortcuts, and continually demonstrated that she was in charge by minimizing the role of the shared service center directors (by this time there were two service centers).

Frequently, she would bypass the service center directors and directly task employees to take actions and complete tasks based on her priorities. As a result of the change in behavior, friction evolved between the shared services center directors and the operations chief. The friction was rooted in our inability to communicate effectively. When the operations chief transitioned to D personality style, I continued to communicate as if she were functioning as she had in the past. My discussions were typically C styled: high details, heavy compliance focus, methodical, and risk averse. The operations chief needed to hear and see that my team and I were on it and we were accomplishing her prioritized tasks. She needed me to provide quick, direct solutions that accepted her definition of a reasonable amount of risk.

Based on positively trending measurable performance metrics, I knew our processes were sound, and I knew my team and I were on the right path. However, my non-negotiable defense of our processes and my demand for the development of higher headquarter-written guidance to accompany the operations chief's directed actions (which I believed were contrary to federal policies) resulted in the operations chief functioning "out of control."[3] Her behavior exhibited signs of impatience, recklessness, abrasiveness, and high stress. In response, my behavior was also nearing "out of control" as I was becoming increasingly inflexible in defense of my team, our processes. For the first time, I began to doubt my leadership abilities, and genuinely became fearful that the chief of human capital, also located in Washington D.C., was losing faith in me.

Had I understood DISC, I would have recognized the change in behavior; instead of becoming increasingly inflexible and defensive of my team and our processes, I would have taken an approach that indicated an increased focus on the operations chief's modified goals. Instead of discussions focused on complex details and compliance, I should have focused on how we would meet the changing requirements with a sense of urgency, and demonstrated optimism in our abilities to reach short term objectives. I also could have accepted a little more risk. By responding in such a way, I would have effectively communicated with a D personality style.

By communicating in the language of a D personality style, I believe the operations chief would have been more comfortable with the direction the service center directors were taking, and would have most likely resulted in the operations chief remaining under control throughout a highly stressful period. By meeting her need for quick wins, for embracing risk, and for being direct, I believe she would have seen the service center directors as partners instead of seeing them as barriers. As a valued partner, the operations officer would have fed my C/S personality style, and thus my needs for consistency, for accomplishing tasks the right way, and for operating creatively would have been met. By feeding my need to be accurate, accountable, analytical, and open-minded, I would have remained under control.

Learning and understanding DISC personality styles was surprisingly impactful for me. It was the first time I learned a new skill, and deeply wished I had understood it and its applicability earlier in my life. Having practiced what I learned through DISC certification, and reflecting on the situation described in this chapter, I am absolutely convinced that the application of DISC Human Behavior theory would have prevented the adversarial, high threat atmosphere that was created. By understanding and using the languages associated with each of the personality styles, relationships will be stronger and trust will be higher, leading to a greater sense of profession-al and personal satisfaction both inside and outside of work.

ABOUT JAMES "JIM" COSTEY

Jim Costey is a servant-focused leader, with over thirty years of leadership experience. Jim retired from the US Air Force, in the grade of colonel. He has served as an HR professional in the private and public sectors, and as a high school teacher. Jim found great success throughout his professional career by focusing on the needs of his teams and ensuring they were set up for success. Jim's learned his leadership philosophy: *Be respectful of all and know that everyone brings value early in life,* and he embraces John C. Maxwell's philosophy of: *Today you got my best, tomorrow you'll get better.* Through those philosophies, his teams have reached high levels of operational success, customer satisfaction, and morale. Jim is a Certified Leadership and Human Behavior Consultant, and began serving as a coach and mentor in high school. Jim holds a bachelor's degree in economics and master's degrees in organizational leadership and design, and in military science. Jim and his wife Meredith are very proud parents of two amazing girls and a pack of rescue dogs. Jim loves cycling and is a rider and fundraiser for the National MS Society. If you are ready to become more, then reach out to Jim at LDRDimensions@gmail.com; www.ldrdimensions.com

Help Others, Help Yourself: Leading Others Through DISC and Its Impact on Our Family Business

Jamie Hansen

We were midway through an unusually difficult winter in Nebraska, and there were indicators that my business manager of two months was about to come unglued...Not over the weather, but over preparations for a leadership conference we would be attending together in Florida. We were scheduled to leave in just two days. Escaping a tough winter for sunshine and warmth is usually regarded as a welcome relief, but that was not the case on this day. Sensing his tension and wanting to help, I asked him what questions he had and how we could alleviate some of the natural anxiety that comes from not knowing what to expect. "They're throwing so much at me, from so many directions, I don't even know what to ask," he blurted back. The frustration in his tone was moving toward exasperation with every word, and I was beginning to wonder if he would be getting on that plane with me in just under forty-eight hours. He continued, "I need context. Clear expectations might be nice too. But with this random spray of ideas and non-sequential information, I don't know how they expect this to be a meaning-ful experience for anyone."

And there it was—the raw emotion he'd been trying to control and even hide from me, albeit unsuccessfully. His words hit me like a grenade, and while I was thinking frantically to form some response, any response, a vision began to crystallize in my mind of me boarding that flight solo and picking out a single window seat, rather than a row of three so he could have a

149

seat on the aisle. My concern was also escalating from whether he would attend the conference, to whether he would even want to continue as Alloy's business manager. Things were not looking good.

Meanwhile internally, I was reeling from his reaction. His words were strong, and each one stung upon impact. There was a ravine between what I was feeling and how it seemed best to respond to him right then. The words I managed to scrape together went something like, "I know you like to have your facts straight. You prepare thoroughly for what you do and get your ducks in a row. This is how you make the most of your experiences and present work that is of the highest quality, and I truly admire that about you. I can only imagine how frustrating this must be for you right now. I felt some of that before my first time attending, and I can also tell you from experience that this group isn't great about providing that kind of information. That's just not the thinking style of their leader or their leadership team. Not that they're wrong, just different.

"Furthermore, to hand over the playbook with its extraordinary experiences and high hopes, especially for first-time attendees, would potentially do you a disservice by not allowing you to experience that for yourself. No filters, preconceived notions, or other people's agendas... This way allows you to see it through your own eyes, and therefore get just what you need out of your time there. Naturally, that means some front-end frustrations for some people, especially the more organized souls among us. So as someone who's attended before, and as your mother, I'm asking you to trust me on this one and make a go of it, even with lots of blanks that aren't filled in right now. Haley is also very excited about this trip and all that's in store, and it will be phenomenal for you two, and your marriage, to experience this together."

Yes, you read that right. My oldest son, Ryan, twenty-eight years old at the time, had recently come on as the business manager for our growing talent development company, Alloy Solutions. The only wisp of time I ever wish I wasn't his mother is when I want to speak with some objectivity about what a considerably good hire he was for us, and what an asset he is to this team. Haley is his wife of nearly five years, a gifted, compassionate physical therapist, and a difference maker in her own right. The good news is that Ryan did accept my request that day to trust me and make the trip—more on that later. That conversation was one of those that could have ended well or ended horribly, with few options in between. They leave you feeling understood, or isolated; closer to one another, or left out in the cold; confident and capable, or confused and inept. We've all had those types of conversations, and perhaps a few of your own might be coming to mind as you read this. Fortunately, that one ended well, and our experience that day is a powerful example of the game-changing impact an understanding of human behavior through DISC can have on business initiatives, relationships, and in our case, the ongoing growth and performance of our family business.

Working with family isn't a concept that's foreign to us. I worked for my father in his grocery store for five years through high school and college, and I still call him "Dave" from time to time, as a playful nod to those days. Our family, the Hansens, have been raising cattle in western Nebraska for seven generations, and currently own the longest-held brand by one family in our state. When our youngest son, Lincoln, was twenty-four, he was pivotal in the structure and launch of our newest business. He was coming away from a successful college football career and looking at his next steps when he announced, "Mom, I have a business degree *and* a psychology degree, and you need help." With that, Alloy was born. We also aren't naïve about the heightened emotional stakes in a family business. The highs can be much higher, and the lows can go much lower. Protecting family dynamics from the demands of the business, and vice versa, does not happen by accident. My experience as a professional counselor is full of tales of couples and families who sought professional help navigating the high and sometimes stormy seas of raising a family while running a business together. I will always admire and applaud those that recognize the significance of their chosen path, and have the humility and courage to call upon the experts to set their families and/or teams up for their best shot at success. Just as our self-deprecating state tourism slogan holds, "Nebraska: Honestly, it's not for everyone," the same can often be said of working with family.

In fact, the nature of our working relationship frequently comes up in the form of questions in conversations with people we meet professionally for the first time:

"How does THAT work?"

"How tough is it working with your mom?"

"I don't think my son and I could ever do that. What made you decide it's a good idea?"

"My daughter and I did that for about a year, and it didn't go well."

"I could see my son being very good at this and I'd love to have his contributions to the business. I just don't know if he'd like to do that."

Their questions usually come with an understandable tone of skepticism for the reasons mentioned above. No matter who answers first, Ryan and I have noticed that our answers consistently involve our understanding and appreciation of each other based upon what we've learned through DISC. We tell them our style blends are basically opposites—Ryan's blend being C/DS, and mine being I/SD. These style blends balance each other out well and make for great complementary strengths when it comes to running the business. We have learned to leverage one another's strengths for tasks, and align our leadership on projects with the needs of the customers we serve. We also know that these opposite blends can become significant liabilities if not managed well during times of stress and/or change. What growing business doesn't have loads of one or both of those at any given time?

We have used DISC with organizations of all sizes, structures, and industries, from the entire staff of a small, privately owned financial services group to the leadership teams at manufacturing plants of global corporations. We have used DISC concepts at keynote speeches for large networking events and industry-specific conferences. Our experience has taught us that whether you get people together in large groups or in smaller, intact teams that work together, it's a very positive audience experience when you introduce DISC. People naturally enjoy learning more about themselves, as well as how they can better relate to others.

Right now, I can picture you and me having this conversation over coffee—on a nice outdoor patio in the sunshine. We've been talking about your work life and mine, and at some point, you say, "This is all quite thought-provoking, and good information to have. It seems like understanding DISC, the way you've described it, could do a lot of good where I work right now. We could use a little help as a team. Unfortunately, I don't own my own business, nor do I work for a family-owned company."

"I'm so glad you said something," I exclaim, and ask you to indulge me for a moment while I put on my professional counselor's hat. Let's talk about families, shall we? Many of us might agree that a family is a group of people that share genetic and/or legal bonds. Basically, you're either born in the family, adopted into the family, or connected to the family through marriage. Relationally speaking, many of us would say that families operate best when they share common values and goals, meaningful experiences, and show mutual support and positive regard for one another. It's not hard to understand, then, why sports teams, especially at the high school and college levels, will frequently refer to themselves as "family." Teams share similar behavioral aspirations for their members as families do, and things just tend to go better when groups of people choose to operate that way. For the same reasons, it's not a large gap to understand why workgroups within organizations often refer to themselves as a "team," and even a "family" in many cases, though they're not legally or genetically related. They see themselves as a group of people that share common values and goals, meaningful experiences, and show mutual support and positive regard for one another. Sound familiar?

Another thought about families before I remove my professional counselor's hat: families are comprised of people; people are imperfect; therefore, families are inherently imperfect. Large or small, families are dynamic and consist of people who can learn, change, and grow. Or choose not to. They are on a journey together, and often recognize that they will never indeed "arrive," but the mission itself is worthwhile, and they will sustain some losses and celebrate some victories along the way.

Families also share a collective blind spot in that they lack objectivity on their behavior as individuals and as a group. As a result, they can be dysfunctional or functional, abusive or nurturing, closed and secretive versus communicative and transparent, neglectful or engaging—or any point along the continuum among these factors. Families are indeed dynamic groups of people. Perhaps this has drawn your thinking to someplace you've worked, or maybe even your current workplace. Terrific—that's the idea. Whether yours is a family business or a business comprised of "families," understanding one another through DISC can have a powerful impact upon yours, just as it has upon ours.

It was day two of our conference in sunny Florida, and that brutally cold winter was continuing to wreak its havoc back home in Nebraska. As we stepped into an elevator, Ryan said, "This has been a great experience. I don't know what I was ever so worried about." I swallowed the "I told you so" that was bubbling to the surface and instead asked him to share why he said that, which he did. It was a very fun and mutually encouraging conversation in the elevator. Even more powerful for me was the thought of what could have happened if I had been lacking the DISC-enlightened understanding of his needs and had reacted differently just a few days earlier. That understanding powerfully changed my tone with him from contempt to compassion, emotional to empathetic, and reactive to responsive. It didn't cost me a thing, and look how much we gained—as individuals, as a family, for him and Haley, and as a company.

That old adage really is true: *You can't help others without helping yourself.* As you've seen in my family's story, I'd like to encourage you with three results you can anticipate when you and your "family" grow together through DISC:

Practical, clear, efficient communication.

Conflict that is more constructive, and less destructive.

The purpose and mission of the business remain the "main thing."

Thank you for lingering over this topic with me. I'd love to share coffee and conversation with you anytime. Until then, here's to you and your family's success, my friend.

ABOUT JAMIE HANSEN

Jamie Hansen is the Founder of Alloy Solutions, LLC, a talent development company that melds your people's industry expertise with proven psychological and human behavior success strategies to optimize your organization's performance. Jamie's twenty-plus years of experience in employee assistance and professional counseling have made her a sought-after leadership consultant, executive coach, and facilitator for many local and national organizations. Through coaching, speaking, and facilitating, she works to develop leaders, engage teams, and add value to the organizations and groups she serves. Jamie believes that a united and empowered group of people can do almost anything, and that belief inspired her to found Alloy Solutions, LLC, with the vision of providing a unique and effective vehicle to help leaders grow and organizations succeed.

Jamie is a Licensed Professional Counselor and is certified as an Advanced DISC Practitioner with Personality Insights. She is a certified Speaker, Teacher, and Coach with the John Maxwell Team. She earned her BA in psychology from the University of Nebraska at Lincoln and her MS in counseling from the University of Nebraska at Omaha.

To learn more about working directly with Jamie, please connect at:

Website: https://www.alloystrong.com

LinkedIn: https://www.linkedin.com/in/jamie-hansen-m-s-lpc-871b5820

Chapter Eighteen

DISCover WHO You Are, WHY You Do WHAT You Do, and HOW to Walk Your Talk

Folake "Dr. O" Oluokun, MD

Is life just all about results and productivity?

Is life just all about inspiring people and building a team?

Is life just all about helping others and building harmony?

Is life just all about doing tasks properly and correctly?

Do you get straight down to business? Do you arrive late to every meeting, including your wedding and even your own funeral? Do you prefer an environment where everyone supports one another and gets along? Or perhaps you are so determined to create an excellent end result that you need to have time to ensure you have been able to check (and recheck) everything...twice.

If you are the type of person who loves getting straight to the business at hand, perhaps it's not that you don't like people, but rather that you are just intensely focused on achieving the goal. If you are the type who is late all the time, perhaps you are just someone who is easily distracted. You might find that you enjoy a supportive environment because you simply don't understand why others would enjoy working or being around drama all the time. Does doing tasks properly and correctly energize you? Maybe you are a "measure twice, cut once" type of person?

Are you aware of why this happens and why it is difficult for you to break free? Have you wondered what is it about you that compels you to behave a certain way? There are many programs out there—tests, questionnaires, and assessments that may give you insights as to why this is. I would like to introduce you to a methodology that is extremely informative and useful in both your professional and personal life. It is based on the study of human behavior, and helping us to understand the predictable patterns behind how and why people naturally tend to act and react the way they do. Before I proceed, let me clarify that this is not about labeling or putting anyone in a box. Rather, it is simply a process to help understand others better, and to build the bridge of commonality that helps to connect us all.

There is a perspective that makes a person bound to the *past* record of thought, behaving, and doing. To be different, each has to stay right on purpose (course) by first DISCovering the meaning of their life. Once someone determines their arrival point, then they must refuse any departure points that do not route them toward their arrival.

This is the same concept that is often referred to as "beginning with the end in mind." A person dreams of a time, place, or situation called "there." The place—"there"—is their dream, place, or situation that they are working toward. Until what one thinks, believes, speaks, and does all agree, they will never realize the things they dream.

Yes, the world belongs to dreamers who are also doers. The only way to achieve this is by taking matters into your own hands and becoming an active participant in your own rescue. There is a saying: "Knowledge is power." You need to understand that knowledge is only potential power. I once heard Les Brown say, "If information was enough, we would all be rich, skinny, and happy." As a medical doctor, I know that many of the health concerns that people face today would be completely avoidable if they just applied the knowledge they already have. Let's face it, I'm here to tell you knowledge without action is worthless.

The DISC Model of Human Behavior is the psychological study of why people naturally communicate and react the way they do. Using this model, we are then able to develop assessments that help us see where on the scale people naturally gravitate toward. The model is divided into four main quadrants. While we are all actually a blend of all four styles, we do have a particular area where we naturally tend to gravitate more than the others. We often describe how each style thinks by using the following terms.

D types think *WHAT?* They want to know the goal that needs to be achieved in order to achieve success.

I types think *WHO?* They want to know who all is going to be involved because let's face it, any time is a good time to have some fun.

S types think *HOW?* They want to know if what is about to happen can be accomplished in a way that doesn't risk causing anyone avoidable stress.

C types think *WHY?* They want to know all the details and that there is a well-thought-out plan before taking action. Also, they need to know the measurable objective...in detail.

1) The D style, which is Direct, Decisive, and Dominant, asks:

So WHAT are we doing right now?
WHAT is stopping us from doing this task?
Their theme is "ready, set, go, go."

2) The I style, which is Intuitive, Impulsive, and Inspiring asks:

WHO are we doing this with?
WHO are our team members going to be to make this happen?
Their theme is to "let the party begin now."

3) The S style, which is Stable, Synergistic, and Supportive, asks:

HOW are we going to address this together?
HOW soon are we course correcting?
Their theme is "can we just get along?"

4) The C style, which is Calculating, Contemplative, and Competent, asks:

WHY is the dream important?
WHY are the next steps necessary?
Their theme is "measure, measure, cut."

As a communication expert, using the DISC methodology allows me to profile and navigate through people's specific personalities. I then understand how each particular behavior style deals with stress, time management, decision-making, and how they react/respond to other behavioral styles. As an individual, by knowing myself and how I respond to situations, this allows me to stop unhealthy thoughts, beliefs, or behaviors. There is power in understanding how your current beliefs will either inhibit, limit, or exhibit your current results. Raising your level of awareness incentivizes you to be more intentional with your thoughts, thus allowing beliefs and practices that create the action steps to become your best self at home, work, and even during your leisure time.

WHAT did I STOP doing because of this information?

WHO did this information help me to become?

HOW did this information change my life at work, home, and recreation?

WHY do I continue to utilize the power-changing tools in my life and business?

The year 2014 was pivotal, marking the tenth anniversary of my bout with thyroid cancer, and divorce. That year, I made a declaration and decision to STOP the BS in my life. The word STOP (Stay True On Purpose) means to intentionally record my personal development by journaling and embracing the journey. The term BS stands for "Belief Systems, Bogus Stories, and Blind Spots." The phrase STOP your BS for a CHANGE is a simple guide for transforming one's current life into the life of one's dreams.

STOP means you must "Stay True On Purpose" in order to remain authentic in your walk. This was a big one for me. I stopped living the life that others wanted me to live. I learned to embrace my faults, my fears, my wants, and needs along with undertaking the task to get to know myself on a deeper level. You see, I no longer live in the shadows and expectations of everyone around me. I am now free to be *me*!

Applying CHANGE is "Creating Habits Affirmations Now Growing Everyday." The only way to create a habit is by repetition: not only by saying these affirmations, but actually doing and being them even when I don't feel like it. Change is always ignited by communicating on the common ground until the connection becomes a conscious, cohesive force in our community transformation.

I am diligently working on changing my BS (Belief Systems, Bogus Stories, and Blind Spots) until my beliefs become more congruent with my true self.

Now, in order to make that transition, let me clarify that your beliefs drive behavior, and your belief systems are just systems that support your belief. Changing your BS or belief systems is not enough if indeed you have not changed what you believe; you will find yourself reverting to what you truly do believe. The DISCovery of my *real* strengths and blind spots added such a tremendous value to my ultimate *real* success in becoming a person of influence that it was worth the effort.

You need to understand that everyone has a unique mixture (what we call a "blend") of all four of the different characteristics found in the DISC Model. This is what creates the whole per-son...We have primary traits that tend to dictate our personality.

For example, physicians are usually more detailed-oriented. Their dominant traits are often the C or D. This is why they are often perceived as cold and uncaring when giving facts/news that is often life changing and emotional to their patients.

My primary style blend is I/D. This is someone who is intui-tive and inspiring. In addition, I am also dominant and decisive. The main reason I was able to navigate from being an I to becoming a physician is that both my parents in healthcare were D and C. My mom changed my perspective to see that structure and order can be positive.

What is interesting is that as a little girl, I wanted to be an actress and a speaker. Due to the influence of my parents, I chose to be a doctor, like my father. As an I, my patients are able to speak to me freely, and I seem less threatening to them because I am a natural talker. I will say I agree with their sentiment. People would say I'm very talkative because I talk quite a bit more than most. I love the arts—acting, choreographing, coaching, cooking, dancing, directing, mentoring, mothering, nurturing, and so forth.

Through medicine, acting and choreographing has enabled me to work with diverse groups of people across the United States—from suburban Maryland, to the Native American reservations in New Mexico, urban areas of Lagos, Nigeria, and Washington DC, rural communities in Arkansas, Virginia, Kentucky, and Indiana. You see, people have a song and a dance that they identify with, and until you hear their song and feel the rhythm of their music in dance, you cannot connect.

As the firstborn, I had to be the example for my siblings, so I graduated from college in a profession which has more inclination for C and D traits. This proves the power of being able to adapt within our personality styles to our environment and to learn to operate within each of the styles of the DISC Model to become whoever we need to be to achieve our desired life. As leaders, we have to be aware of our giftedness and challenges. In our giftedness lies our inner awareness of strengths that enable us to understand self and influence others. Within our challenging problems lies our perception of our blind spots that will allow us to understand others, and how they respond to us.

ABOUT FOLAKE OLUOKUN

Born in London, United Kingdom.
Raised in Lagos, Nigeria.
Resides in Greenbrier, Arkansas.

As a DISC Human Behavioral Consultant, Certified High-Performance Coach, and emergency medicine physician, she empowers REAL CHANGE in the lives of her clients and patients.

As an Executive Director with the John Maxwell Team and a member of the JMT since February 2014, she was one of the coaches who qualified to join The John Maxwell Leadership Foundation initiative for Nation Transformation in Paraguay in 2016, and Costa Rica in 2018.

She helps individuals DISCover and maximize their strengths and minimize their weaknesses to STOP (Stay True On Purpose).

Dr. Folake Oluokun (for-lark-ay *ohh-loo-ohh-koon*) is affectionately known as Dr. O to her clients and friends, Momma O to her children and family and, as of March 2019, G'Momma O to her grandson Zeke and granddaughter Jonelle. She's a single parent to her most favorite daughter, Debbie, and her five sons (including two stepsons).

As a cancer conqueror since 2004, Dr. O runs her RACE with GRACE like a RACE horse that's RUNning to WIN.

www.folakeoluokun.com

www.WumanOnWaya.com

www.STOP4aCHANGE.com

Chapter Nineteen

Houston, We Fixed the Problem

Gary Belzung

"Houston, we have a problem." I bet you think you know the whole story behind this iconic phrase, right? Well, you might know what the 1995 movie *Apollo 13* told you about what happened 200,000 miles from earth on April 14, 1970, but let's look at what happened long before John Swigert ever flipped the switch that would forever imprint this phrase in our minds. We now use this phrase anytime we foresee something about to go wrong, or when we get hit with a problem we can't seem to solve.

Years before Jim Lovell actually said, "Houston, we've had a problem," NASA brought on multiple teams of designers, several manufacturers, hundreds of engineers and technicians, and even a team of back-up astronauts for this mission. It was all these multiple teams that solved all the problems that brought Apollo 13 safely home. What NASA had done was to prepare teams to solve problems before they even knew what problems would occur. So, what does this have to do with DISC, you ask? Building a team with lots of different skills and personality behavior styles before unexpected challenges or emergencies occur is essential to the success of any business, not just NASA. But the big problem with building teams is selecting the right people for it. Often, people will build their teams with similar personality styles, because they are comfortable with their personality behaviors. Understanding DISC teaches us that the behavior patterns we don't have, want, or usually wouldn't even think of doing ourselves just might be the very behaviors we need around us to complete our team.

Stacking our teams with all four personality behavior styles will ensure we have the skills and personalities it will take for success, no matter what unknown challenges jump up in our future. Can you imagine a business that had only accountants?—no salespeople, no production people, and no customer service people. What about a business with only salespeople? There would be no one to verify profits, no one to manage all the daily details, and no one the take care of the problems. By adapting our vision to see what's important to all our current and future customers/clients, we can bring on team members to reach most everyone, and more importantly, to be ready to solve challenges as they arise.

So, you're thinking, how could this ever apply to my world, right? Well, my journey with DISC started before I ever even knew what predictable human behavior was. In 1987, my wife and I joined with another couple to start up a youth camp for our church. Youth camp was something that had shaped us as kids and teens, and we wanted others to have the same experience. Although none of us had ever done anything like this before, we jumped in and started the process. We all worked hard and put in a lot of hours to make it happen. After a couple of summer camps, I began to notice that while I was running around busy doing stuff and working my tail off, others were just sitting there watching me do all the work. We needed to get ready for the kids—and there was a lot more work than one person could do—and there they were, just talking and laughing. Frustrating! I felt like they were just lazy, and I just could not understand why they didn't get up and help me! What I didn't know at the time was they were busy building relationships that allowed them to reach the kids and become impactful in the lives of our young campers. They too were baffled, but at me, because I wouldn't stop all the busyness to take the time to understand the kids and build relationships. They were thinking, "All that stuff will get done, but reaching the kids is more important right now." They too were frustrated that I couldn't see what was really important at that moment.

After a couple of years of being frustrated, I began to look for help. I attended a seminar after that second camp, looking for a way to fix everyone. As the speaker began to describe me and my thoughts over the past two summers, I was wondering if someone had told him about me. The speaker then began to describe the actions of my lazy group, and one of those epiphany moments happened. He said something I already knew, but just couldn't seem to relate to the situation I found myself in. While I know he didn't actually say my name, what I heard was, "Gary, you can't change anyone but yourself." He went on to explain the difference between a "task-orientated" person and a "people-orientated" person; neither was right or wrong or needed fixing. My view of the world and the people around me changed that day. Just a few minutes after the personality style mystery had been revealed, I could clearly see that we needed "task-orientated" people like me to get all the stuff done and in place, but we also needed the "people-orientated" people to build relationships and reach the kids. I learned to adapt my vision of what is important and necessary by seeing youth camp from both perspectives.

As it turned out, the other couple and I are all task-oriented, and my wife is a people person. As you can imagine, this led to some, let's say, "lively" discussions at my house those first two years of camp. I remember taking separate cars to events for a while so one of us would be on time. If you're a tasker, you know exactly what that means, if you're not—you'll never understand. But I learned to adapt my vision and adapt what I let be important. My life has now become best described by the recent country song, "Waiting on a Woman." But that's a story for another time.

Learning to understand DISC fully, and the predictability of human behavior, allowed us to start and run a youth camp in 1987 that is still going on today and functioning very well. By making an intentional effort to learn how to find and include all four personality styles in all areas of my life, I was also able to run my own architectural business for twenty-five years and help two other architectural firms build better functioning leadership teams. I know you and your team will become more successful as you begin to do the same.

Of course, team building the DISC way is much easier to talk about than actually put into use in our daily life. Maybe you don't think you have all four of the DISC personalities available for your team. But to know that, you would have to have all your people complete a DISC Assessment, right? Oh, you think you may know a person's true DISC style, but most people learn how to become the style they need to be in order to function at work, or at home, or when with friends.

If you were one of the kids at our one-week-long youth camp, or a visiting parent for our parents' night, you would bet money that I am a high I, because I learned to be very social and talkative, as well as flashy and comfortable being in front of the crowd. I also tell stories when I teach and use wild, messy examples to help everyone learn the point of the lessons. But, if you went through the nine monthly training sessions before camp, as the camp staff did, you would see me as a High D, because I took charge of every meeting and was very direct and blunt in our training. I was also very driven about reaching our set goals for each monthly training session. In reality, I'm a high C...very detail-oriented, very organized, and I overanalyze almost everything. Those closest to me will tell you I seldom express any emotions, and rarely smile. My DISC style blend is CS/D. My I is actually my lowest personality trait. Over time, I learned how to adapt my outward style to become what was necessary to fulfill what was required. You and your staff have learned this also, even if you're not aware that's what you all are doing. By having you and your current team, and any new hires, complete a DISC assessment you will really know what your team's DISC styles are, and the potential your team might have, as well as the blind spots you may not know about yet. Having the right people on the correct team is what will amplify your team's communication and effectiveness.

Each Personality Insights DISC Assessment provides you with a very detailed report of the predictable human behaviors associated with your specific personality blend of the four DISC personality styles, including two different personality style graphs. Graph one is your "Environmental Style," which gives you the specific personality style blend you have adapted to in order to function in your daily world. Graph two is your "Basic Style," which shows your real, specific personality blend when you are in your most natural state. Your report also shows you how to communicate and interact with the other personality styles that are not like you, which if you're a High D, is 90 percent of the people around you every day. When you understand the predictable behaviors of your individual team members, you can then adapt your communication style so you can connect with each one in a manner that they will receive and understand. But the real benefit is when your whole team learns how to do this. I can speak from experience about how the team dynamics can change when a team begins to use the DISC Human Behavior concepts. Our youth camp team quickly became the ministry everyone at our church wants to be a part of, and the two architectural firm leadership teams that I helped are blowing past all their team goals. I know that learning, understanding, and putting the DISC principals into action was a major factor in these teams becoming so effective.

The kicker in making the shift from any theory to action is the buy-in required, along with the initial work needed to get everyone up to speed at the same time. You know that feeling you get when you step on a people mover at the airport—that sudden jolt, and a burst of speed? That's what buy-in feels like. If you've ever stepped on a people mover, that sudden jolt can be quite a surprise, and you usually need to grab the handrail to keep from falling. Even if you've been on one before, it's always a noticeable jolt when you step on it again. Getting your team to step on the people mover is the key to shifting from theory to action. You should know that changing the direction of an existing team is like turning a barge; it takes more time and energy than you might expect. It won't happen overnight, or in a week, or after a single training session. When a team starts moving, it creates friction, which heats things up a bit. Oh, then there are your High S team members. They absolutely despise change. They will need much longer to buy in to the change than anyone else on the team, so start early with them. My suggestion is that you bring in a DISC facilitator/trainer who has the skills to help you and your team turn that barge.

As DISC facilitators and trainers, we hear many leaders say: "I don't need this DISC stuff" or "I'm just a small business" or "It's just me, I'm a one-man show here" or "We're too busy to stop for that kind of training; we have too much to do every day." My personal favorite is: "We'll worry about that when we get bigger." Henry Ford is credited with saying, "If you keep doing what you've always done, you'll keep getting what you've always got." If you are no longer satisfied with what you're getting, it may be time to change what you're doing. It's never too soon, and you're never too small to start using the DISC principals. The sooner you and your team understand the predictable human behavior styles and how to spot them, the sooner your life and business can change. Jim Rohn said, "If you want things to change, you have to change. If you will change, everything will change for you." I learned a long time ago that you always start planning from Point B back to Point A. That holds true for a lesson you want to teach, running a successful business, and getting a spaceship back to Earth. NASA prepared for unknown challenges so that when that fateful call came in, they would be able to complete their mission. Instead of always telling Houston that you "have a problem," are you prepared to start saying, "Houston, we fixed the problem."?

ABOUT GARY BELZUNG

Gary Belzung began his leadership and personal growth journey in 1987. Since then, he has devoured personal growth and leadership materials and hasn't stopped. He has attended over 100 seminars and training events, as well as studying over 300 leadership and personal growth books.

Gary believes every leader should make a difference in this world, and over the last three decades he has trained, coached, and mentored dozens and dozens of leaders who have, in turn, raised up their own leaders. He became hooked early on with helping emerging leaders learn new skills that catapulted them forward in their careers and personal growth. Even though he's made his living as an architect since 1975, he's made a difference by pouring the leadership knowledge and wisdom gained over his career into the folks who are moving into new leadership roles.

Now that he's retired from the architectural world, he's moved into his last career, doing the thing that brings him the most joy—coaching, training, and mentoring leaders. His legacy will be the leaders that he pours energy into and then go on to raise up more leaders.

Gary's website: https://www.gbaleadership.com/

LinkedIn: https://www.linkedin.com/in/gary-belzung-39863a5a/

Facebook: https://www.facebook.com/GBAleadership/

Chapter Twenty

Never Fear! Super Me Is... Has Anyone Seen My Cape?

Pamela Quinn

I'm not exactly sure at what age the perception of destined greatness came into my awareness, but I don't remember a moment without it. I knew I was going to do amazing things and everyone, I mean everyone, would know my legacy. Not just local newspaper kind of legacy, but history book worthy. I had early visions of "superhero" moments where I soared through the air to save the day with my cape flying behind me. But with the inevitable onset of realistic thinking, I sought more practical ways to become "Super Me"—cape optional, but highly recommended.

I was aware of each unique opportunity. From Little League softball to gymnastics, and playing the piano for church; the Olympics, Broadway—I was born for the big stage. All it would take was the right person to be there at the right time, and I would be discovered. The world would finally know what I was capable of. I wasn't particular about where the point of my success might land; I simply knew it would land at the highest possible level.

Coming into middle school, I realized most prodigy legends have been discovered by this age. I began to consider that my gifts would serve at a different level. I recall during a career discovery session, I had written down that I wanted to be a CEO. I didn't know what those letters stood for, but I knew that person was in charge, and that's where I was heading.

Fast-forward to that first significant leadership role. Certain traits had taken me on the fast track to being the youngest in the room. I was bold and ambitious. I didn't let conflict or risk deter me. By the time I landed in that room, I was certain I belonged there.

One of the other traits that I brought to the table was a very unique ability to clear the room. Many of the traits that landed me in the room of leaders—most fifteen years or more my senior—suddenly had a more adverse effect. But honestly, I didn't mind; they would all come around eventually...My previous positions had been ones where I worked either independently or led a team toward a common goal. I was sure that I would be equally successful as part of a team; they just didn't yet realize how incredible my contributions would be.

Fortunately for me, there was an individual who noticed my struggle and pulled me aside. She acknowledged my intent, my goals, and my potential in our first conversation. "She knew!" I said to myself. But in that same conversation, she shared the barriers she saw me creating within the team. The words, actions, and manner in which I contributed were building walls that would eventually be too strong to be broken through. Through her wisdom and desire for my ideas to make it past an empty room, she guided me. I was able to understand that I needed to engage in a way that allowed others to join, not just follow, and to ask questions and consider how to incorporate others' ideas. She would guide me along by pointing out success in meetings with good outcomes, and helping me discover a better way when meetings would end in a stalemate. Eventually, with her guidance, we became an innovative team working together to serve and grow. She had gently and respectfully found my cape, though I didn't yet understand I needed it to soar.

As with other positions, I sought more, and eventually pursued the license I would need to lead in this field I fell in love with—skilled healthcare. Graduate school was a good testing ground for how I might lead independently once again. The setting served me well, and I was ready to transition. In fact, the room I once cleared through my direct and abrasive approach even gave me my first desk plate— "ADMINISTRATOR" —as I left for my next adventure.

The first team in my career as an organizational leader was an absolute gift. They were diverse and hungry. The various skills and traits they brought to the table were perfect for an environment of growth. Because they had struggled with securing a strong and decisive leader for several years, they wanted those strengths I could so easily deliver. Together, we created absolutely incredible systems of service and exceeded all growth expectations. Ironically, I did this all without someone guiding me, helping me to see the best decisions, words, or approaches. In my opinion, I had arrived. The growth we achieved was soon noticed. I was approached with new opportunities and made the difficult choice to leave the incredible group of people I had dubbed my "Dream Team." Little did I know how much I had needed every single one of them to achieve the level of success we attained.

My next leadership adventure did not have an "instant team." I set out to create another dream team in my new setting. In the process of hiring, I was drawn to those who I enjoyed speaking to, had the same drive and instincts as I did, and were inspired to inspire others. I created a dynamic team ready to take on the world! There was one problem. None of us had the patience or interest in reading the map to find that world. Any time we found ourselves remotely close, we struggled to find common ground for growth—there were too many ideas. We had incredible fun, and we had great potential, but we had limits.

And then there was the one interview, the one I really didn't enjoy—a bit dry, not very inspiring, but functional. At the time, I needed functional. That one new hire changed the trajectory of our team and our company, and helped us build beyond the limits we had previously been held to. This individual's attention to detail, focus on function, desire for security, and more closed a gap in our wheelhouse, letting us roll upward toward heightened success. For the next several years, that one person found not only my cape, but also the capes of many others, and with our joint contribution as a team, she too found hers. We could soar together.

Fairly quickly, our soaring experience acquired a different feel. There was some rubbing, some pushing, and some conflict. In my journey to uncover how to sustain what we had achieved and move forward well, I discovered DISC. After the first training, we felt like we had just been reintroduced. Newfound friends with a mutual respect for styles, contribution, and gaps, we secured a more effective relationship. In fact, the training held such great impact we introduced DISC-based communication training to all layers of the team. We even wore our style proudly on our name tags so that we could secure each other's capes well along the journey.

In reflection, I found the ongoing awareness of my personal style was key to advancing each step of the journey, even back in the day when one of my greatest skills was quickly clearing the room. The peer who took me aside wasn't sharing with me a task or technical skill: she was sharing a better opportunity to secure influence based on who I was, and who those were in the room. Her knowledge and awareness were an incredible gift, not only to me, but also to those who served alongside me. As for that "Dream Team," sometimes we just get lucky! In looking back, we had a perfect blend of visionaries, risk takers, influencers, supporters, and detail trackers. The balance was perfect. I was merely the right funnel (thanks to my amazing teammate previously showing me the way!) to allow their gifts to flow effectively and successfully.

You might be thinking, "Wait, we started talking about the 'big stage' of Olympics and Broadway and landed here in the business realm? How did this happen?" My awareness of vision, risk, and potential were inherent. It was part of who I was. And while it seeded in my youth as visions of the big stage, it manifested in my professional growth and desire for that CEO role. That second team I mentioned was truly my team. I acquired operations of the struggling organization at the age of thirty, and built it into a multi-million-dollar asset in just a few short years. But the most significant asset throughout this journey was found in the relationships, and I mean the type of relationships where one can confidently find and secure another's cape so that everyone can achieve greatness in the end.

In the DISC Human Behavior Model, I am a D/I. My D and I are so heightened that my gaps aren't subtle. Not only do I often leap without my cape, I frequently don't recall where I put it. It's hard to leave the kind of legacy one finds in the history books when you don't take the time or attention to secure all of the necessary resources. While I continue to pursue that legacy, I now have an awareness of the need for accountability partners and strong team members. These individuals will help me evaluate the full situation and capture the details before I leap. C types and S types are essential to my success and effective growth. D types and I types are great thinking partners to create ideas that impact lives and influence outcomes. The opposing gifted individuals complement your strengths as well. Knowing who they are and embracing them in your inner circle is a critical step to embracing your true superpowers.

As my awareness of DISC increased in the professional field, I quickly discovered that I was floundering in my ability to create a living legacy in other areas as well. One of my children mentioned their chore list looked like a decorated professional contract. It took me back a bit to hear a twelve-year-old bring my professional work into how I managed my roles at home. At first, I dismissed the concept. But as I prepared the bullet-pointed chore and activity list for the following week, adding in the spring graphics and colors, I realized he was absolutely right! There were no connecting points, recognition, or relationship gains in the process. In fact, I had it set up with clearly directed task descriptions to avoid any need for dependence or clarification. It was posted, chores were done, and we were moving on to other things. With a husband also a strong D, it was our children that helped me find and secure my cape. They enabled me to best serve, engage, and teach those we were blessed to raise along the journey. With six children, we spent a great amount of time helping them find their capes as well. We would secure their cape so they could soar beyond the challenges they experienced, and build relationships and foundations for their future.

Do you remember that team I mentioned? The second one where I brought on people who I enjoyed speaking to, spending time with, and working alongside? We certainly had our challenges when we set out to change the world. Our team made great strides when we finally added a member that could fill the gaps we held naturally. At home, I had also chosen a spouse I enjoyed speaking to, spending time with, and working alongside. And as you can imagine, that didn't always lend itself well to a productive relationship. In fact, we were both strongest as Ds. Being a D/I and my husband a D/C, we were both very much in charge, plotting the course, and taking control of each step of the journey. I was looking for the next cliff diving adventure, and he was looking for the next investment. When it came to interpersonal relationships, that wild passionate love that brings people together could easily become buried in tasks, schedules, and responsibilities. Neither he nor I were highly sensitive to the personal needs of each other, and we struggled with listening and compassion. Parenting was also a great challenge as we approached both communication and consequences differently. In the end, it was simple awareness that allowed each of us to find our cape in a dignified manner, quietly held up by one another in those critical moments of need. That same awareness will enable us to be intentional with our words, our actions, our purpose, and the people we love.

We all hold a destiny for greatness...a big stage, a key role, the right place and right time situation that will let us shine and create a legacy for the history books. We have within us a "super" power, a gift unique to us, but no one is meant for the journey alone. We all need someone to help us secure our cape along the way. Awareness is the key to embracing those who will hold that role, and in turn, doing the same for them. Together we are better. Your legacy is now. Lead well.

ABOUT PAMELA QUINN

Pamela brings twenty-plus years of sales, operations, and business experience to the services offered through Lead Your Legacy. Prior to acquiring a healthcare operation, Quinn excelled at bringing challenged programs past barriers, and implementing transformational training systems. These systems secured individual team members' commitment to ongoing change and growth. Under her leadership, organizations experienced an average 300+ percent growth in key performance indicators during the first year. Key strengths include securing marketplace opportunities for workforce and client base, mission-based systems, and culture evident business environments.

As an established entrepreneur, Pamela has developed concepts and strategies to inspire cohesiveness among professional peers, vertical and horizontal team relationships, and community leaders. The foundation of this cohesiveness lies in the "legacy" impact of action, leadership, and communication. In pursuit of expanding the footprint of the legacy leading concept beyond healthcare, Pamela established Lead Your Legacy in 2016 to guide others to embrace their role as a leader and pursue the legacy they are intended to lead. Pamela is an Executive Director with the John Maxwell Team and serves on the President's Advisory Council for this international organization. Utilizing the resources of the John Maxwell Team, Personality Insights, and more, Pamela Quinn secures the best training and system development opportunities for clients. To learn more about working directly with Pamela, please connect at:

Website: www.leadyourlegacynow.com

Chapter Twenty-One

Living the DISC Life!

Melissa Rollins

WOW!!! This is how I describe what DISC has done for me in my life. For me, DISC has had a profound effect on my family. I only wish I had known of this model when my children were younger. DISC has helped me learn why I react to things the way I do, as well as showed me how I am naturally wired. For the longest time, I hated that I was so sensitive to what seemed like everything in the world. Once I understood that was how I was wired and that it was okay, I just needed to accept that, but also know when I may need to adjust to other communication styles. Understanding myself was great, but going a step farther and learning how different communication styles are wired as well opened up a whole new world to me. I learned that some people do not talk as much as I do, or use big gestures, or even are as loud as I am, and that is okay. I learned that some people are faster in pace and talking and generally functioning in life than I am. I have also learned that there are people who are way more task-oriented than I am. I am working on that adjustment in my life. I am a very people-focused person—everything I do is usually for someone or to help better someone—but I see now where the tasks in life, in general, are critical as well. I have now learned that this perspective is very important to task-oriented people, and I need to honor that need in their lives.

I remember when my oldest son was young, and he would ask soooooo many questions...ABOUT EVERYTHING! I had no idea at that time why he asked so many questions; I just wanted it to stop. Now that I understand DISC, I completely understand why he asked so many questions. He had a need that had to be met for his communication style. He is very task-driven and reserved. He wasn't just asking questions to ask them: he truly needed the answers to those questions. If I would have known that back when he was younger, I believe I could have felt so much less frustration towards him. Life would have been so much easier for both of us had I known these things back then. He is now grown, and we have a great relationship; he has even learned about DISC through his father and me, and has learned to use it in his own work environment.

As for my marriage, my husband and I are so much alike in some ways, yet so different in other ways. We are both very outgoing, but he is also very task-oriented, and I tend to lack in that area. He is also a very bottom-line type of guy. I would sometimes interpret this as rudeness, or him being mad at me when he would be short with me about something (at least, that's how I was taking it). I have come to learn that it was just his communication style, and my sensitive nature taking things wrong. It was another learning moment for me; he wasn't mad at me at all. Usually, he was just in the middle of something and was so focused on the task at hand that he just wanted to answer me and get back to his task. Understanding that he is very outgoing and task-oriented, whereas I am very outgoing and people-oriented has been an eye-opener, especially when you look at how we are so much alike, but yet still so different at the same time. We have always had a great marriage, but I honestly believe understanding DISC has taken our communication and relationship to an entirely new level.

My youngest is even more high energy than I am. As a child, he would wear me out. It was so hard to keep up with him; it seemed as if he was always on go and didn't even want to stop to go to bed at night. As I learned his communication style, I became aware that he is very outgoing and yet very people-oriented as well. From one moment to the next, he would go from being all about doing things himself, to wanting to climb up in my lap and snuggle, to helping out his friends. I admire how strong he always has been, but yet how tender he could be as well. As a teen, he saw the value in learning the DISC Model of Human Behavior himself and asked to go through the training. We took him through both the basic and advanced levels of certification, and he took that awareness with him to college. It helped him understand his professors better, as well as his fellow students, which helped him communicate with them at a higher level. He is now in the Army, and he is using his knowledge there as well. It is incredible to see how understanding the psychology of human behavior can benefit us all. People are amazed at how he communicates with others around him who seem so utterly different from him. It is all learned, my friend!

I think once we understand ourselves, it makes it so much easier to start understanding others and learning to adjust to their communication style. Notice I didn't say *change*, I said *adjust*. When you are high energy and outgoing, you cannot expect a reserved person to have the level of energy and outgoingness (what we refer to as the "Motor of Activity") that you have. When you are extremely outgoing, you may have to learn to lower your pace and voice and speak to others in their style. The same thing applies for reserved people, though. You have to be willing to raise your energy level and your volume when you are speaking to someone who is outgoing. These are learned traits. Although it is not always easy at first to adjust, it is not impossible—you just have to be aware. The same thing goes for people who are very people-focused. Task-oriented people can often be perceived as unloving people, but that is false. They love people; they just show it through tasks. To someone who is task-oriented, a people-focused person may appear to lack focus on the task itself, but they have to realize that *people* are their task and focus. It's a fantastic dance once you understand it all. I have always said you cannot change something if you are not aware that it needs to be changed.

Before I became a DISC trainer, I had to learn about me, and it was such an eye-opener. I was not broken, and I did not need to be fixed...I just needed to understand myself better. I now tell everyone, "If you are breathing, you should know DISC." I say that because of the enormous effect it has had on my life, and the life of my family. I now communicate effectively with them, whereas before, I was just communicating. It has also helped me to communicate with the clients in our business more effectively. We love helping people grow their businesses and grow themselves with what we have learned through DISC.

Now that I am a DISC Master Trainer, I love to see people in our classes that either know little about the model, or have had some exposure to it. To watch the classes over the two-day certification and the understanding that starts sinking in is one of my all-time favorite things. Day one is where we lay down the foundation of the DISC model and help them understand it. Day two is when I see it really start to sink in, and they start to actually relate it to their daily lives—be that their home life, work life, etc. I love when people start to say, "*Ooh*, that's why I do that," or even better, when someone shares, "Now I understand my kid," or "I think this is going to save my marriage." That is what makes it all worth it—helping people understand themselves and others, and watch them take what they have learned back home, to the workplace, to church, or wherever. Communication is what we all do to one another, but effective communication is something we can do with each other. Listen, really listen to what people are saying, so you know how to communicate back to them in the way they truly *need*.

Once you have been trained and you are now aware, you have to remember that not everyone is aware. We cannot expect the people we communicate with on a daily basis to adjust to us. We are the ones who are aware, so it is our responsibility to adapt to them. Think of it this way: if you were bilingual and met someone who spoke one of the languages you did, but not the other, would you expect them to try to speak in the language they did not understand? Of course you wouldn't. That would be silly, wouldn't it? Since you had a proper understanding of how to speak both languages, you would simply adjust and speak to them in the language you both understood.

Well, DISC is just like that. When you understand the four languages of DISC, you can use this knowledge to connect with anyone. It is a universal language. We have worked with, trained, and certified DISC consultants from every continent across the world. It is incredible to see this commonality that we all share. Remember, this is a learned process though; it doesn't just happen. We have to be willing to learn and then implement what we have learned. For me and Chris, this has just become a way of life. We are so passionate about it...how could we not teach it to our kids and the hundreds of people we have taken through training? WE BELIEVE IN THE IMPACT IT HAS!

How many times have we said, "So and so is so rude all the time," "She is such a snob," "He asks too many questions; just be quiet already," or "She never shuts up."? Did you ever stop to think that the problem here might be that you simply do not understand how to speak their language based on their communication style? Think about this: the Golden Rule says, "Treat others the way you want to be treated." We have all heard that, right? That is not a bad thing...We all want to be treated nicely, and we should treat others nicely too, but what if we take that a step further? What about the platinum rule? *Platinum rule?* What's that? "Treat others the way *they* want to be treated." You can replace "treated" with "communicated" too: "Communicate with others in the way they need to be communicated with." If, once we are educated in the DISC Model of Human Behavior, we would just slow down a little and really observe people with a trained eye, we could help them at a higher level. Often, outgoing and reserved traits can be seen in people quickly and easily, but what about identifying task- and people-focused traits? If you really start to listen to what people say, you can begin to pick up on the signals they are putting out. If they are saying things like, "I feel" or "I think," these are two signs we can use. When someone speaks in terms that relate to "feeling," it can indicate they are more people-oriented. When they speak in terms that relate to "thinking," it can indicate they are more task-oriented. Now that is not 100 percent foolproof, but it does help you to get a feel for where they may lean, in terms of people- versus task-orientation. Those who are people-oriented tend to be more emotional, and those who are more task-oriented tend to be more cognitive in their thought- and decision-making processes.

If you are outgoing and loud, do you want to receive communications for very long from someone with a monotone voice and low energy? NO! Because that would wear you out. The same goes for someone who is more reserved...That individual would be worn out by someone communicating too loudly and very animatedly all the time. When we are aware of how we communicate, we can do it more effectively. Communication is natural; we do it every single day. We talk, but do we listen? There is another side to communication as well. We communicate with each other, but are we being effective? I challenge you today to educate yourself and to become a better communicator, whether that is just at home with the family, or at work with co-workers, in your own business with your clients, with your customers, or someone you just happen to meet on the street. If you would like to inquire about training with us, or about our live, two-day certification sessions, reach out to us. Now, go out and communicate with purpose on purpose!

ABOUT MELISSA ROLLINS

Melissa Rollins is the Vice-President of Rollins Performance Group, Inc., where she uses their proprietary 3C Model of Performance to help companies achieve massive organizational growth by focusing on developing the foundational principles of effective communication, connection, and conversion skills.

Through her impactful keynote presentations and workshops, she shares her story to serve as an inspiration to others by delivering a simple, yet powerful message. "Don't let your past dictate your future." Her delivery empowers people to move forward from the circumstances of the past and into a future that they desire on their way to achieving the full potential that already exists within their unique giftings.

Melissa is a Master Trainer in the DISC Model of Human Behavior who loves delivering the live training experiences that she and Chris host throughout the year. She enjoys creating special experiences for the participants, helping them learn how to apply the information received in the "real world" when they leave. She hosts certification classes for those who want to become certified, and better yet, qualified. To learn more about working directly with Melissa, please connect at:

Website: https://www.rollinsperformancegroup.com

LinkedIn: https://www.linkedin.com/in/melissarollins1/

Chapter Twenty-Two

Where Do We Go Now?

Chris Rollins

Congratulations! As you have read through this book, you have learned from some amazing experts who have shared practical ways that they apply the Model of Human Behavior known as DISC to help a wide variety of people and organizations from all walks of life. Our goal from the beginning was straightforward; we didn't want to write a collective book where everyone wrote about understanding the model of DISC. As I mentioned in the opening chapter, there are plenty of books available today that already cover that. If you want to read a book that discusses the DISC model in detail, and gives outstanding examples of each style, I highly recommend you pick up a copy of *Positive Personality Profiles* written by Dr. Robert A. Rohm.[1]

Our collective work was intended to demonstrate how this model is applied in all walks of life. We often discuss the drastic difference between teaching people an academic model that is merely informational, versus teaching them a model that can be applied directly in their daily lives. Whether you are a stay-at-home parent who is raising children, or you are working in a nonprofit, in education, government, fitness, the corporate world, a church, or in the sales world, this model applies to you. And yes, the consultants who contributed to this work use validated assessments that can help you begin to take the next step of your journey. We have a variety of assessment types available. There are children's editions that are developed in a story format for those in the five- to twelve-year-old range. There are teen editions for that age bracket as well. We offer multiple adult editions as well. Assessments vary based on the amount of information you want to receive, from a six-page concise report all the way to an incredible sixty-three-page leadership version. We also have specialty fitness, and sales versions as well. As good as the available reports are, allow me to explain where the real difference comes in. You might be reading this and thinking, "We've taken assessments in the past, and nothing really changed." I couldn't agree with that statement more. In fact, during my corporate leadership career, I felt like taking some new assessment each year was the norm. Let me walk you through my experience and see if you can relate to the following scenario.

The human resources department has just sourced a new assessment and forwarded an email with the link to take your very own unique assessment. Don't worry, they know it seems like you have received different assessments every single year for the past fifteen years (like a broken record), but this one promises to be *different*. They are truly excited to provide this one to you. They ask you to complete it as soon as possible, but you have a lot more pressing deadlines on your plate and a boss who is far more concerned about the results you need to produce than taking the time to complete an assessment, so you open it up, spend fifteen minutes or so completing the answers (all while dealing with the other "urgent" email notifications, phone calls, text messages, employees walking in with an immediate need, etc.), and finally click the submit button. You see your instant results and are rewarded with your report. You hit the magic print key, pull the paper off the printer, look at it for a couple of minutes, then staple it together and put it in the drawer with the rest of the assessments you have collected over the years. You go back to work and, as long as you finished it before some pressing *deadline*, you probably never hear from anyone again... Well, at least not until next year when the newest shiny object arrives in your inbox.

See, I told you I could relate. After my time in the military as a tank commander, I spent sixteen years overseeing large sales and operations teams in the rental industry across multiple states. I know how Fortune 500 firms operate. Now, allow me to explain where the flaw is in this process, and then clarify what you need to do to avoid the same time and money wasting result.

The fatal flaw in this process is that people rely on an assessment to create cultural change. You can take any assessment you want (ours included), and it may provide you with some great insight and information. However, to fix the flaw and tap into the real power of an assessment, you need something more than a mere report. My friend, the power of any assessment is never found in the written information itself—it's in the trained eye of the person who is able to help you interpret the information the report provides, then help you develop clear, actionable steps based on your unique report, following a proven process. Let's face it, the information you needed to learn during your formal education was already provided in a textbook. What you needed was an instructor who was well versed in the subject matter you were there to learn. Only then could you move from conceptual knowledge to practical knowledge.

I encourage you not to overlook the statement I just made because it seems simple. I teach my audiences across the country that success is often overlooked and missed due to its simplicity. It takes hard work, but the process is not complex. Both ends of the spectrum often look at success from a skewed perspective, causing a huge disconnect. On one end, the people who are trying to attain a level of success are often busy chasing the complex and hard-to-understand concepts. The logic they use is that it must be complicated, because if it were simple, then everyone would have already achieved it. The principles are usually right in front of them the entire time, but because of their preconceived ideas, they overlook them and dismiss them. They are like the teenage kid who walks in a room to look for something, turns a circle, then yells, "It's not in here." Then the parent walks in and points right to it, sitting on the bed. Any of us who have raised kids can completely relate to that. On the other end of the spectrum, leaders often feel like they need to make the process of success sound like they have done intensive research when they teach others. They feel like they have accomplished their goal when the audience is blown away by all the incredible information they shared. Too often, the crowd leaves with the assumption that the presenter must have been the smartest person in the room because what they shared was so intense that it went over most of the heads in the room.

Listen up, leaders; your job is not to leave people thinking more highly of you after you interact with them. It is to leave them thinking more highly of themselves. When they think that you must be brilliant because they could hardly keep up with what you said, you might impress them, but you are not helping them. I remind leaders often that you cannot seek to help people while seeking to impress them at the same time. Some decisions in life are truly either/or. Your job as a leader is to seek to help people. As Jack Welch shares, "Before you are a leader, success is all about growing yourself. When you become a leader, success is all about growing others."[2] When others listen to you and then realize *they* are capable of achieving greatness, they leave empowered and then...you truly are brilliant! See the difference?

Explaining things in this manner has nothing to do with *dumbing it down* for others. It has everything to do with putting concepts out there is such a way that others can receive the information, process it, internalize it, and then put it into action. Only when the information we share with others becomes actionable and duplicable does it lead to sustainable success. As Albert Einstein said...

If you can't explain it simply, you don't understand it well enough.[3]

This is why it is so important to connect and work with people who have been well trained, and are qualified to help deliver the training and resources you and your team will need to move to the next level. It's why I said in the introduction that there is a big difference between someone being certified, and actually being qualified to help you. I have seen firsthand the number of people who call themselves DISC Certified when all they really are is a glorified affiliate out to sell some assessments. No offense, and I don't say that to sound harsh, but I am a High D/I style, so I often speak very directly. If all someone can do is offer you an assessment and perhaps a token session, they aren't equipped to help you provide the cultural shift you need to be able to skyrocket your results.

Before you wonder if I am implying that taking an assessment is not an important part of the process, stick with me as we continue. Yes, you need to complete an assessment. The important thing is to realize that the assessment is only the first step in the process and is not intended to be a comprehensive strategy alone. Three things will make working with a qualified DISC Consultant effective. It is paramount that all three of these criteria are met if you want to get the highest ROI from the investment of your time, effort, and resources.

Training

Hands down, this is the most important aspect to look for when determining whom you are going to work with. Personality Insights Human Behavior Consultants like the ones who contributed to this book attended multiple days of live, in-person training sessions to ensure they had an excellent working knowledge of not only the DISC Model of Human Behavior, but how to apply that model in the real world as well. We don't give them scripts to read from when they work with you. You are looking for an expert, not a parrot. We completely understand that. Many of our consultants have gone on to take additional training and become Advanced Accredited Consultants as well. Besides that, they often continue utilizing hundreds of hours of ongoing learning and development in addition to teaching the DISC model to companies, teams, and families across the world. This universal model has been tested on every populated continent of the world. In short, I wholeheartedly believe you couldn't find a better collection of people to work with.

Curriculum

One of the things that I believe makes those who are affiliated with Personality Insights, Inc. stand out more than anything else is the wealth of curriculum resources that have been developed for them to use over the years. DISC is not a "We did that once" type of training. Just like establishing a strong safety culture, or a culture of service or sales, successful programs require the development of a strong sense of practicality, and of being able to utilize concepts in everyday examples of business and life.

These contributors have resources that have been developed, tried, and tested over the past three decades. If you are looking to teach your team the fundamentals, they've got you covered. What about getting along with others, learning to present effectively, managing your time, learning to listen effectively, along with building leadership, sales, and stronger teams, as well as reducing conflict, or even working with students in a classroom environment? Yep, they've got you covered with all of that too (and then some). To date, there are already over twenty-five different curriculums developed that can provide need-specific training for your teams, and they range from a couple of hours to a full day per topic. The curriculum continues to be enriched over time as well. While I have seen several companies in the DISC marketplace provide quality assessments, and a few of those that offer a good training process, I haven't seen anything that even comes close to the wide selection of excellent resources that a Personality Insights Certified Human Behavior Consultant can offer you. It is the main reason I have associated myself with them, and why I only certify consultants in association with the Personality Insights brand.

Assessments

As explained previously, while assessments aren't the highest thing on my list, you need to ensure that you use a brand that can provide quality, validated assessments that have been studied and proven reliable by the Cronbach's Alpha standard. Listen up! I have asked people who offer different personality assessments to show me their validation studies. I have also received the response that "DISC has already been validated." Do not be misled by that statement. Yes, DISC as a science has been researched and validated. It is not flawless, but neither is any science that deals with human behavior. The ingrained flexibility of the model honors the fact that we are all unique. Its intent is to help us understand people better, not to put them in a box; however, just because a psychological model has been validated, it does not mean an assessment has been as well. The science's reliability and the assessment's reliability are determined independently. If you use a flawed assessment related to a proven human behavior model, you will still receive faulty feedback.

Any of the consultants in this book can provide the specific study of the assessments we use to put your mind at ease, and let you know that the resources you are utilizing when you work with them meet exacting standards to achieve statistical reliability.

In Conclusion

Ready to change the culture of your organization, team, church, or even your family? As I'm sure you have already realized from the people you have learned from in this book, you are in the right place. If one of these authors was the one who provided you with this book, reach back out to them—do yourself a favor, and get started on working together. If you would like to know more about going through the comprehensive training process with us to become a Certified Human Behavior Consultant in association with Personality Insights, then let's connect. We would be more than happy to discuss getting you set up and ready to join us at one of our upcoming, live training sessions. Until next time...

"DREAM BIG!!! Then take MASSIVE ACTION!" - Chris Rollins

ABOUT CHRIS ROLLINS

Chris Rollins is the founder and president of Rollins Performance Group, Inc., a company that focuses on developing leadership and sales teams to achieve massive top- and bottom-line growth.

He is also a veteran M1A1 tank commander and platoon sergeant. During his sixteen-year corporate career, he led high-performing sales and operational teams in the rental industry, where he became known as "The Sales Train Conductor." He uses his experiences to help his clients learn how to challenge "in-the-box" ideas and concepts in order to achieve "out-of-the-box" results.

Through his impactful keynote presentations, seminar and workshop sessions, books, or consulting clients one-on-one, Chris uses his proprietary 3C Model of Performance as his foundation. The model focuses on the elements of Communication, Connection, and Conversion as the keys to achieving consistent and sustainable growth.

Chris is a Master Trainer in the DISC Model of Human Behavior who has spent thousands of hours studying human behavior and teaching the model to others. He hosts certification classes for those who want to become certified, and better yet, qualified. To learn more about working directly with Chris, please connect at:

Website: https://www.rollinsperformancegroup.com

LinkedIn: https://www.linkedin.com/in/chrisrollins1/

ENDNOTES

Chapter One

[1] "The origin of soft skills", Joe Wright, February 17, 2018, https://code.joejag.com/2018/the-origin-of-soft-skills.html

[2] https://www.goodreads.com/quotes/7494681-85-of-your-financial-success-is-due-to-your-personality

[3] https://www.brainyquote.com/quotes/nelson_mandela_121685

[4] *"The intellectual content is provided with permission by Dr. Robert A. Rohm & Personality Insights, Inc.* www.personalityinsights.com, *and copyrighted - All rights reserved - Duplication is prohibited.*

[5] Ibid

Chapter Three

[1] https://www.nps.gov/moru/learn/historyculture/gutzon-borglum.htm

Chapter Six

[1] https://recruitloop.com/blog/much-can-disengaged-employees-cost-business-infograph

[2] https://www.livescience.com/59349-knowing-yourself-helps-your-understand-others.html

[3] *The How of Wow!* John J. Murphy

[4] https://www.brighthubeducation.com/teaching-methods-tips/128391-different-types-of-learning-styles/

[5] https://trainingmag.com/trgmag-article/2018-training-industry-report/

Chapter Seven

[1] "What Matters More to Your Workforce than Money," Dr. Andrew Chamberlain, January 18, 2017

[2] ibid

[3] http://www.enrich.org/blog/The-true-cost-of-employee-turnover-financial-wellness-enrich

Chapter Nine

[1] Kelly, Donald C. December 11th, 2017|Categories: Blog News, Sales Success

[2] Selling With Style, Personality Insights, 2014.

Chapter Twelve

[1] Proverbs 27:19 https://www.biblegateway.com/passage/?search=Proverbs+27%3A19&version=NIV

[2] John C. Maxwell (2019). Leadershift: The 11 essential changes every leader must embrace. Harper Collins Leadership.

[3] Quote from Gabrielle Bernstein https://www.brainyquote.com/topics/reflection

[4] Robert A. Rohm (1992-2018). Positive Personality Profiles: Discover Insights into Personalities to Build better Relationships

[5] African Proverb "If you want to go fast go alone. If you want to go far go together." https://www.passiton.com/inspirational-quotes/7293-if-you-want-to-go-fast-go-alone-if-you-want

[6] John C. Maxwell. The 17 Indisputable Laws of Teamwork: Embrace Them and Empower your Team (2001). Thomas Nelson Publishers. Nashville Tennessee.

Chapter Fifteen

[1] https://www.personality-insights.com/disc-profiles-2/

[2] Kilbane, Clare R. and Milman, Natalie R. "Teaching Models: Designing Instruction for 21st Century Learners." Pearson Education, Inc. New Jersey, 2014.

[3] Maxwell, John C. "The 21 Irrefutable Laws of Leadership." Nashville, Tennessee: Thomas Nelson, Inc., 2007.

[4] Rohm, Robert A. "A+ Ideas for Every Student's Success." Atlanta, Georgia: Personality Insights, Inc., 2006.

Chapter Sixteen

Resources

https://www.huffingtonpost.com/eric-sheninger/the-essence-of-a-leader_b_10951604.html

Large Flip Chart, Personality Insights Inc.

Adult Profile Personality Assessment & Guide, ©2017 Personality Insights

Funbook, Discover How to Understand Yourself and Others, ©2015 Personality Insights

[1] Emotions of Normal Peoples, William Moulton Marston, © 1928, Kegan Paul, Trench, Trubner & Co. Ltd New York: Harcourt, Brace, and Company. https://archive.org/details/emotionsofnormal032195mbp/page/n7

[2] Personality Insights, Inc, *Adult Profile Personality Assessment & Guide*, © 2017

[3] Personality Insights, Inc, *Funbook, Discover How to Understand Yourself and Others*, © 2015.

Chapter Twenty Two

[1] https://www.personality-insights.com/shop/positive-personality-profiles-overview-of-disc/

[2] https://www.brainyquote.com/quotes/jack_welch_833427

[3] https://www.brainyquote.com/quotes/albert_einstein_383803

WANT TO GET CERTIFIED?

Ready to go in-depth on the DISC Model of Human Behavior?

Our comprehensive training certifies you as a "Certified Human Behavior Consultant" in association with Personality Insights. When we made the decision to become Master Trainers, we had a strong desire to ensure that the people we trained were equipped to make a positive and lasting impact for their clients. There are three things that we heavily considered when we decided to certify DISC trainers with Personality Insights.

1. Training – Certain elements of the DISC Model can be taught online, but when you are learning to identify different aspects of human behavior, nothing compares to learning in a live setting where you experience the differences in real life by sharing the room with people of various styles. This is why we reject the "online training" certifications in the marketplace. Our sessions are two full days in an in-person, interactive setting.

2. Curriculum – Creating content is one of the most time-consuming aspects that a trainer faces. Imagine having over twenty-five different pieces of pre-developed curriculum available at your disposal that ensure your ability to serve your client's needs. Each booklet provides what you need to host half-day to full-day sessions. Well, imagine no more. All of the material is also available to consultants at wholesale pricing.

3. Assessments – Personality Insights uses validated assessments offered in six different adult versions, not including the teen and children's versions that are also available.

What makes taking the training with Rollins Performance Group different?

- We conduct all of our sessions in small group formats. This allows us to provide personalized attention to each participant and address questions continually throughout the training. It's an experience you will not find in large group training sessions.

- Our participants can join our private Facebook community where they can communicate, share ideas, and seek feedback from other DISC trainers long after the training session is over. Our members consistently tell us that the support received within the community is priceless.

- You can only process so much in a two-day time span, so we focus heavily on the interactive portions and on the application of the model while we are together. However, we didn't want the training to end there, so we host weekly recorded teaching calls. To date, we have over 150 hours of teaching calls available to our members. Our single goal is to ensure our members are the best equipped in the industry, bar none!

Want to join us for an upcoming session? Visit us at: www.RollinsPerformanceGroup.com for more details or to register for an upcoming class. Come experience the difference for yourself!